Devil's Sport
My Perilous Journey Into The Darkness

BEATRIX SZANTO

Burning Bulb
PUBLISHING

Devil's Sport: My Perilous Journey Into The Darkness
By **Beatrix Szanto**

Burning Bulb Publishing
P.O. Box 4721
Bridgeport, WV 26330-4721
United States of America
www.BurningBulbPress.com

Cover designed by Beatrix Szanto.

First Edition.

Paperback Edition ISBN: 13: 978-1-948278-19-5

Printed in the United States of America.

Beatrix Szanto (Bea) is a sincere and heartfelt being who has experience with various religious denominations. Her personal experience with spirituality has played a huge role in the way she guides and counsels' others. This has stemmed from both strong beliefs in faith as well as wanting to help others around her. She has had countless supernatural divine experiences with faith which has been witnessed in multitudes by me and many others.

Bea resides in New England in a small Connecticut town with her kids and husband. She is an outgoing and empathetic person who is well liked by her co-workers as well as many of my patients. I have been working with her for a couple of years now and consider myself blessed to have crossed paths with her.

—Michael Lund Sr. Physician Assistant
MONSON, MA

I have had the pleasure of knowing Beatrix for about six years now. She is very in tuned spiritually and when my husband passed away two years ago, she rushed to my aid to comfort me. She has an extremely calm presence and wears her heart on her shoulder. She never had the opportunity to meet my husband Jeff and yet she was able to share an unbelievable insight about our life together.

One thing in particular that blew me away was her knowledge about the purchased headstone and the special engraving on it. A week after the installation of the tombstone I ran into Bea again. She pulled me to the side and informed that Jeff, my deceased husband is delighted with his headstone. This was very emotional for me to process at the time but it helped me to heal tremendously.

She no longer practices mysticism and has actually reformed to a fully committed Christian. It seemed to happen abruptly and when asked what the reasons behind her conversion, she simply said "the truth has been revealed to me and I have been deceived in the worst way possible." I didn't understand the specifics but I can attest that a once psychic/medium is now an extremely devoted lover of Christ.

—Kelly Cleary, Manchester, CT

I have known Beatrix since high school. Our journey in life has taken us in different directions but that didn't stop us from crossing each other's path throughout the years. I have been blessed to have had the opportunity to experience several spiritual experiences with her. She is a very attentive, understanding and easy to connect with no matter what the occasion.

On one particular night she came to my aid when I was in desperate need of advice and emotional support. What I experienced that evening still lingers with me today. She has helped me to heal my emotional battles in more ways than one. I was shocked to learn that she no longer practices energy healing and or psychic readings but at the same token I respect her decision. I have no doubt and truly believe the horrific accounts that she encountered as she has always been a true and honest person. Her integrity has always been consistent and reliable.

—Betsy Moure, Groton, CT

From the time I first met Beatrix six years ago to where she stands now in her life is absolutely amazing. She has influenced me greatly and has helped me to reconnect with the Lord above. Her spiritual confidence is impressive and has gained the attention of many. I truly believe that her gift is being used for God's will and a purpose to help many others. I feel honored to call her my friend and hope that her testimony will lead as a great example of strength and courage.

—Justine Morin, Chicopee, MA

ACKNOWLEDGEMENTS

I cannot express enough sincere and heartfelt gratitude towards my dear friend and mentor Michael Tourville, who gave me the courage, direction, knowledge and dedication to complete my book. This book would have never come to fruition without his patience, guidance and persistence. You will remain forever in my heart and soul. I would also like to give a special thanks to Gary Lee Vincent who decided to take upon himself to help publish my book after reading it on a whim with such short notice. I am grateful for his generosity and risk taking with aspects to investing in my story and helping me with the manuscripts professional polish.

Although the content of the manuscript is mine, without the help of Michael and Gary, my book would have never been able to reach the far and few who need to relate so they don't feel isolated with their similar experiences. Especially to those that need to stumble upon my book in hopes of shedding light on their deception and veil.

I would also like to give an extended thanks to my loving pastor, Father James Parnell, whom quickly came to my aid when I needed it the most and who accepted me and continues to do so in a non-judgmental way. His children's love towards me have been a blessing in more ways than one during liturgical services. To my friends and co-workers who offered to read the rough draft and provide feedback in a kind and friendly manner. I appreciate them taking the time out to help with my project. I am deeply touched by the many people that I randomly came across, who not only expressed much interest and compassion towards my experience but as a result helped to ignite my first thoughts and ideas of actually writing this book. They inspired me and gave me the confidence to continue to speak up about my revelation and helped me not to feel ashamed and disclosed.

Finally, and foremost, my appreciation to my family, including my most supportive and durable husband, Todd Fox. His love, patience and commitment gave me the emotional support that I undeniably needed during my times of fear, struggle and frustration. I suffered many bouts of anxiety and fear during the time which it took to write this book. Although he never fully experienced the demonic attack, he sure was a witness to what unfolded yet didn't leave me stranded but rather helped to keep a close eye out on me during my healing process. I have been blessed to have him in my life and hopefully with many more years to come.

PREFACE

Trust in the Lord with all your heart and lean not on your own understanding;
in all your ways submit to him, and he will make your paths straight.
(PROVERBS 3:5-6)

I have been resisting the call to write this book for quite some time now, but with God's gentle persistence, I made way and surrendered to our Lord and Savior's will. I was adamant to complete my book project not only as a huge token of appreciation for coming to my rescue, but in the hopes of possibly saving the many other souls that are currently lost in the world of new age and mysticism, also known as modern day paganism.

On December 25, 2017, I was baptized as an Orthodox Christian, for God had saved my soul once again. However, this wasn't just an ordinary form of baptism because things were going to be very different going forward. It seems God had bigger plans in mind and ordaining me to preach my true personal experience in order to expose the devil's sport behind the works of psychics and mediums was just one of many.

Throughout the book you will not only get to know me personally, but you will also be given the chance to be bought to a whole new level of knowledge, awareness and enlightenment with regards to how the enemy (Satan and his legions of demons) works behind the scenes within the spirit world and the cruel deception and trickery he tries to use in order to bait human souls.

I decided to expose my truth for a multitude of reasons, most importantly to help others who are deep in the new age movement to understand just how easily the devil hides behind the invisible cloak of mysticism and spirituality. The second most important reason for writing this book is in the hopes that another soul might be saved, even if the devil already branded their soul. By the end of this book you will be able to recognize God's true light versus the devil's lie and learn

3

how to flight and flee from the addictive psychic world, so you can un-slave yourself and hopefully attain salvation.

When asked what this book is about, I simply say; this is a true story of me and my salvation, and how God mercifully delivered me from the hands of the evil one. I have truly survived a saga that most people wouldn't even dream of encountering, never the less, be able to handle. My direct goal is to not only caution others but to possibly prevent another from becoming a victim.

DEDICATION

I dedicate this book wholeheartedly to my Father and creator, his son and Savior Jesus Christ, and of course the Holy Spirit. I am also dedicating my writing to Father James Parnell, who played a very important role with my journey to redemption. I truly believe that God utilized him as an intercessor on behalf of my salvation. Without the trinity and God's grace, I wouldn't have been able to receive the guidance, protection and forgiveness that I immensely and urgently needed. Thankfully with the Lord's patience and divine intervention, I was able to obtain forgiveness and be completely healed from the trauma that I experienced. Because of this, I will forever sustain my faithfulness to the Lord.

In the name of the Father, the Son and the Holy Spirit
GLORY TO JESUS CHRIST

Amen

CHAPTER 1
THE PRECOCIOUS CHILD

Where it all Began

Born in Budapest, Hungary in 1976 and later entering the United States as an immigrant in 1985, my life began with some definite challenges. The biggest of them was not being able to speak one word of English as my family and I stepped on American soil. I was at the tender age of nine and the influx of immigrants from different parts of the world was at an all-time high. I don't know about my mother and step-father, but my brother and I experienced a lot of backlash and prejudicial stigmata during those times. My brother Attila was only seven years old at the time and the fact that we were living in poverty quickly classified us as outcasts.

I wore the same clothes day in and day out which I'm sure contributed to the teasing and the bullying that my brother and I had to endure on a daily basis during school. We lived and took refugee within a poor area called "the ghetto" in the city of Hartford, located in Connecticut. I dreaded hearing the school bell dismissal, for I knew the cat and mouse game all too well. While others were living lavishly, for us, white rice with fried eggs was usually our main course of meal in the evening and breakfast mostly consisted of cereal and or farina. Our small apartment was located on the third floor within a three-family house but that didn't seem to stop the cockroaches from infesting our tiny living space.

My mother, whom I still call *Ma,* was short just like her mother and carried a type of hairstyle that was always short and curly. Although she worked painstakingly hard to put food on the table, I very much resented her heavy smoking habit and the suffering migraines I would endure because of it. Her piercing blue eyes constantly reflected pain and I remember her crying a lot, especially in the mornings. Granted she tried to hide it, inside I knew that she was suffering in silence. I'm sure the adjustment of the culture shock was just as intense for her as it was for me, but she never did express it verbally of just how vulnerable and frightened she must have been. Her constant sadness confirmed my suspicion either way. I can't recall my step-father working during those times, for he turned out to be nothing but a bad memory. At the time, I didn't know that we were being sponsored by a church congregation who supported new immigrants but considering the circumstances and the age that I was at the time, I wouldn't have been able to comprehend it anyway. I never did get to know who that church was, but I will be forever grateful, that's for sure.

Unfortunately, I don't seem to have much recollection of me and my life in Hungary and I have always questioned the mystery behind it. Most of the memories that I do have before leading up to our departure from my homeland to the United States consists mostly of my grandmother, whom I always called Mama. I faintly recall the small apartment complex that she lived in, which consisted mostly of red bricks. The sidewalk and its surrounding landscaping consisted mostly of stone pebbles, not tar or concrete. I think it was a senior based gated community because the environment always seemed quiet and subtle and her neighbors all seemed to be of old age. I was told later by my grandmother (Mama) that my mom would bring me and my brother to her quite often, so she could watch the both of us while my mother worked.

My sweet grandmother, who only wore dresses, loved her clear seltzer water, specifically the one that she had stored in a silver colored metal spritz can. I still remember giggling at the bubbling water and the way it would suddenly come bursting out. There must have been a playground nearby because I remember my brother and I playing there frequently. Although these recollections seem far and few, at least they were good ones. Anything before that is non-existent as far as my long-term memory goes, which in theory, according to psychologists and other experts is an induced form of amnesia that is triggered by our deep-rooted internal defense mechanism, especially after experiencing severe trauma. I will never know if that was the case, although I highly suspect it, and at this point in my life I really don't care to know either way. It's been said many times, what's left behind is meant to stay behind and for good reasons, and I truly believe this to be true.

My biological father's name is and or was Attila and he never seemed to be in any of the pictures we took as a family. I say "is" or "was" because honestly I am reluctant to say whether he is still alive or not, as I do not know for sure. According to my mother's staggering stories, he abandoned us soon after my brother was born, which might have been a blessing in disguise, for he was not only an alcoholic, but physically and mentally abusive towards my mother throughout their entire relationship. Nevertheless, he was very much into body fitness and competition, which explains the photo that my mom has kept of him. All jokes aside, in that photo, I swear he looks like an Italian version of the incredible hulk. He was a handsome man at best, whom, according to my mother, fell short to infidelity numerous times during the relationship. How sad, that to this day, she still can't bear to look at the photos that are left of him without getting emotional and teary eyed. The photo that I just mentioned is the only memory I have of him, which logistically is just a physical trait. Non the less, he must have left a huge scar on my mother's heart because no sooner than he left, she fell in love with my devil of a stepfather.

While my struggle to adjust to the new change was just beginning, it was also during this time that my step-father maliciously started to sexually abuse me. I am not going to go into the details of the abuse, mostly because that part of my experience is irrelevant to this story; however, I do feel the need to mention it because it was during those times when my search for God officially began.

As you will come to know my story, you will see how my reckless search for real genuine love led me on a destructive path which ultimately led me to expose myself to people, places and things for all the wrong reasons. I do remember picking up the bible at a very young age, and although I couldn't really read at the time, I still very much enjoyed looking at the pictures of Jesus and the heavenly looking animals that were in the portrait with him. I especially enjoyed looking through the Jehovah witness's watchtower pamphlets, the ones that we use to get every week in the mail.

Living in a home that did not believe in God's existence surely added to the chances of me rejecting the Lord, yet I still took much interest in the complexity of the bible, which I think was pretty extraordinary considering the odds. Or was it? Maybe God was already calling me subconsciously, for he knew of the evilness that lied within that household. My grandmother played a huge roll in me wanting to learn about the existence of God and his love for mankind but most importantly she gave me the hope of a better life which I so desperately longed for at the time. Her love for Jehovah became quite apparent, thus she was already a faithful follower of the Jehovah witness's domination and has been for many years.

I later learned that my grandmother and my mother had a very turbulent relationship in the past and that my grandmother abandoned her temporarily for a couple of years when she was a young child. This made me sad because this wasn't the grandmother that I knew and experienced during my youth. Despite all this, she obviously must have loved us unconditionally because for someone to endure almost eighteen hours of travel time overseas (one way) in order to visit with us here in America, is nothing short of pure love. Her visits would only last six to eight months at a time due to her visa restrictions, but it would be during these intimate times that she would relentlessly ask the same question, and always in a soft loving tone; Beajachka, (nickname for Beatrix) don't you want to live with me in paradise forever? And of course, I always answered yes, for her eyes weighed heavy with much sincerity and compassion.

Sadly, the last time I saw my Mama was in 1997, after my daughter was born. I wish I had known that she was never going to return, for I would have spent more time with her. Although she seemed to be forever gone physically, spiritually her influence would stay with me for many years to come. M*ama* suffered from severe dementia until the age of ninety-two, and a short time before she had passed, I sent a cross medallion to the nursing home in Budapest, Hungary where she was being cared for, with the instructions to never take it off the wall until she passed. My grandmother passed away peacefully on December 24, 2018. I still think of her often and miss her dearly. I have prayed desperately many times to God asking for him to grant a seat for her in heaven, which she very much deserves. The fact that she passed away on Christmas Eve gave me the assurance that God granted my request and answered my prayer. I believe that the Lord used that specific day because it has much relevance to me, as you will see later in the book. God tries to communicate with us even if in an unusual manner and I'm convinced that this was one of those times. He was essentially saying, "don't worry, I heard your prayer and your grandmother has made it to heaven."

***

The Visit from Grandma

A couple weeks after my grandmother's death I experienced an encounter which I believe was my grandmother confirming her passing into heaven. It was my day off from work and I was sitting on the sofa watching television. It was around 1:30 p.m. on a Thursday afternoon and the weather was rainy with a dark overcast. The window shades were pulled down as usual in order to block the outside glare that was constantly directed onto the television screen. Suddenly, to the right of me a large yellow beam of light emerged as if someone had just turned a bunch of flashlights on, all at once. My son was sitting to the left of me and noticed the odd occurrence. I got startled and jumped up from the sofa and opened the window shades thinking that maybe the weather suddenly turned very sunny and somehow the outside light peaked through. As I looked out the window, I saw that the sky still had a dark overcast with fog and rain, just as the weatherman had predicted earlier that day.

A sudden calmness overcame my fear and I instantly knew that my grandmother was checking in on me from the other side. Before this occurrence, I cried over my grandmother's death daily, but since the encounter, my grief ceased entirely.

CHAPTER 2
THE SUBJECT OF AN EMPATH

*Be alert and sober in mind. your enemy the devil prowls around
like a roaring lion, looking for someone to devour.*
(1 Peter 5:8)

From a young age I have always felt different and misunderstood. I
have never felt a sense of belonging in my existence; thus, I have always
felt homesick to a world unknown, to a world beyond this one. I have
always been known as the sensitive one, especially to the pains of life
and its brokenness and according to my delicate soul that was never
going to change. Being abused as a young child, I'm sure added to these
immense emotions and feelings, but what I would discover later
proved otherwise.

Between the age of ten and eleven, I was already being taunted by
frightening dreams and suffered extreme episodes of night terror. As I
set forth into my teens, accounts of the paranormal and its existence
was experienced often. This strange awareness included me seeing
flashes of white lights shaped like stars to my name being called (always
in the right ear) to unexplainable episodes of sleep paralysis and
spiritual attacks. I will never forget the time when my bed slightly
shook back and forth, as I am sure, the entity intentionally wanted to
make its presence known in a malevolent fashion. I firmly believe that
this entity continuously tried to inflict the fear of evil upon me
throughout my childhood and into my maturing years so that I could
be instilled with fear. I was alone and isolated, and my family never
took much notice. Besides, they wouldn't have believed me either way.

There were many other unexplained paranormal experiences and
occurrences that I would later endure, and it didn't matter where we
lived or moved to, this thing was relentless. I dreaded going to bed
because I knew that during my times of sleep a spiritual assault would

most likely occur. The phenomena always transpired in the following manner.

- Dosing off to sleep, although not fully awake, I would still be aware of my surroundings. This altered state of consciousness would slip me into another realm or dimension, where I believe demons can dwell.

- While weaning in and out of consciousness, I would immediately become aware of an evil presence in the room. Although I could not see it, I knew very well that it was there.

- Feeling paralyzed by my knowing of what was about to happen next, I would desperately try to wake myself out of the twilight sleep, but I never could because my mouth felt like it was taped shut and muffled. Even if I did wake, once I fell back asleep the attack would resume.

- Eventually I would flee the entities grip but not without having an out of body experience first which always seemed to dissipate but the impact of the memory always left me feeling sore, as if I had been physically attacked the night before. The following day I would always experience lethargy and a migraine, and my chest would feel sore as if I had just run a marathon.

By my mid-twenties these experiences became less frequent, but the constant nightmares of the devil trying to possess me became notably evident. It came to the point where I could no longer sleep with the lights off, in hopes that the light would deter whatever was haunting me. Unfortunately, that didn't stop the nightmares and the aggressive psychic attacks. At times I would feel utterly defeated by the recurring experiences, but I also knew that there was something different about me, and that I was being pursued by the spirit world for specific reasons. During this time, I knew absolutely nothing about spiritual warfare, although the 1973 movie "the exorcist" taught me otherwise. The movie's factual events seemed to secretly resonate with me in a frightening way, and in time I would get the answers as to why. To this day I still cannot and will not watch any movies that are based on possessions and or exorcisms.

Feeling frustrated many times over, I felt like my experiences were never going to go away. One summer night during one of my intrusive dreams, I suddenly had this urge to call on *Jesus Christ* for help during the attack and with it came this unexpected surge of spiritual strength that would ultimately lead me to announce the following: ***"In the name of Jesus Christ! I demand that you go back to where you came from, go back to your place of hell, in the name of Jesus Christ!"***

This worked instantly, making the demon dissipate immediately. These experiences gave me the realization that there was something very serious going on with me and my spirituality, but on a lighter note, I steadily started gaining resilience towards the demon's attempts to subdue my soul.

As I entered my early thirties, my haunting experiences seemed to become less intrusive, but my extrasensory perception, intuition and clairvoyant abilities did not. In fact, my psychic dreams and visions of insight were now slowly and surely beginning to emit into the outside world. My friends and acquaintances also started to take much notice, but I remained shy and a skeptic, at least until my late thirties. As a matter of fact, I didn't fully embrace my extraordinary capabilities until age forty.

Once I gave in it felt justifying to know that there really was a rhyme and reason behind my spiritual suffering, and suddenly life seemed to make a little more sense. Swiftly, I grew not only confident but excelled as I became arrogantly competent with my gift, only to be later lured into the hands of the evil one.

CHAPTER 3:
MY JOURNEY THROUGH RELIGION

But there were also false prophets among the people, just as there will be false teachers among you. They will secretly introduce destructive heresies, even denying the sovereign Lord who bought them, bringing swift destruction on themselves.
(2 Peter 2:1)

Before going into the nuts and bolts of my life as a psychic medium, I think it's important for me to share with you the ins and outs of my experience with religion and how it impacted the choices I regretfully made. I am not here to judge the variations or the rights and wrongs of other religious beliefs; I am just simply sharing my personal experience and opinion about the matter. It is not my intention to offend anyone but rather to inspire and educate. Despite it all, I believe that I needed to experience my story, for had I not, I would have never stumbled upon God's light and truth.

As mentioned earlier in my introduction, my grandmother and her love for Jehovah not only inspired me but led me to my first hands on experience with religion. I was fourteen years old when I became involved with the Charles Taze Russell movement also known as the Jehovah's witness denomination (Charles is considered to be the founding father of the religion). Despite Jehovah's promise, I became discouraged once I learned that their creed forbids the celebration of Christmas, birthdays and certain major holidays. Also, their rules on the forbiddance of blood transfusions and their reasons behind it just didn't agree with me. Don't get me wrong, I loved Jehovah's purpose and my grandmother's teachings about the faith, but their principles just couldn't surpass my struggle of comprehension.

At sixteen I fell in love for the first time and ended up being lost in faith for a few years. I was constantly running away from home and the darkness of my childhood memories. Feeling desperate to break free from my past I was looking for love in all the wrong places.

At nineteen years of age I started dating a guy named Yusuf, we weren't very far into the relationship when I got pregnant.

Throughout my pregnancy, I would seldom read scripture, but my hope in God and his existence was still very much on my mind. On April 13, 1997, I gave birth to a ten-pound baby girl which kept me consumed and very much distracted as I was now a first-time mom. God seemed absent for a short time but that was far from the truth because I know he was still very much tugging, shaping and molding my restless heart as you will see through the progression of my journey.

While at home on maternity leave, a group of Mormon missionaries found their way to my door. They seemed extremely passionate about their faith, and by the third visit during a bible study session, my consideration into Mormonism became official. It was new and exciting, and I was ready and eager to learn the ropes. However, the more I tried to grow in their "Restorationist Christianity Movement" the less I became intrigued with the traditions. Besides, I could never compromise to their rules of banned tattoos and body piercings. Mormons are also prohibited from drinking caffeinated drinks, which meant no coffee. Yikes! I did still make an attempt to stop drinking coffee, but to no avail. This particular rule of law seemed absolutely ridiculous and I just couldn't break away. Besides, nowhere in the bible does it say not to drink coffee. I slowly started to disengage myself from the bible study group, meanwhile, my daughter's father and I separated. This forced me to move a few towns over and after I relocated, they never reached out to me and I never reached out to them. That was the end of my relationship with Mormonism.

At twenty-two I was a single mom who was desperately fending for survival. In the fall of 1999, I finally landed a full-time job working as a medical assistant in a surgeon's office. The surgeon, whom I won't name, was a native from India who ended up becoming a father-figure in my life for a short period of time. He was also affiliated with the Hindu religion and its practices, and so for the next three and half years I fully submerged myself into the academic studies of Hinduism. I read numerous books based on dharma, atman, karma and their righteous way of living. Meanwhile, I still believed in one apostolic God. Sounds messy, doesn't it? Well it was. I even tried meshing the two together, which was merely impossible. Yet I still went forward with the occult.

The new job and my newly formed paternal like friendship invigorated my soul and gave me the motivation to succeed in my new role as his right hand. I remember thinking, wow; so, this is what it is supposed to feel like to have a fatherly love. I was exceptionally thankful for this new connection and a few years into working there I decided to get my first tattoo. I was in love with the friendship and had the utmost respect for him and wanted to prove my loyalty by branding myself with ink. He even offered to choose the ink style for me, and with stupidity I accepted, because it seemed very pleasing to him at the time. Within a couple of weeks, it was decided that I was going to get the "Om" symbol. To the Hindu population, the Om symbol is like the cross to a Christian and although I didn't quite understand it's meaning and what it stood for, I went ahead and got the tattoo anyway. What can I say, I was hopelessly in love with our father daughter relationship and I was desperate to keep it that way. In all honesty, at that given time, I was ready to convert into a Hindu even if I didn't even care to believe in it.

As the year came and went, the fire that I had felt in my heart for Hinduism dwindled and I eventually left the job for a higher paying position. I really felt compelled to increase my income because I was constantly struggling financially and could barely make ends meet. I gave my two weeks' notice with sadness and excitement and although I was going to miss him terribly it was time for me to move on.

In the year 2000, I acquired a couple of workout friends at the gym, who belonged to an association called "Shin-Buddhism". The people within the association always seemed calm, cool, collected and easily approachable which made me instantly like the teachings it offered. I eventually earned my acceptance and ended up becoming a full-fledged member within a few short months. Keeping my vulnerability in mind, I instantaneously took a liking to the traditions and admit that I was not only intrigued, but allured by their peaceful presence and the beautiful temple they held their worshiping in. I was also the youngest member in the group at the time and recall feeling quite flattered when I gained the attention of the seasoned elders.

I was even allowed to bring my daughter to the temple since I was a single mom at the time and had absolutely no help in the babysitting department. Nevertheless, for the first time in my life I felt fully confident and somewhat at peace with myself and with the dark memories of my past. Plus, I loved the meditation with the chanting sessions, mainly because it seemed to help subdue the anger and the frustration that I was harboring all the time. I am positive that most of the anger stemmed from my feelings of betrayal and the resentment that I held towards the senseless inflicted suffering we as humans are forced to endure. To no surprise, my thirst and hunger for the truth was still left unmet and in within a year I weaned myself away from the temple and the practices of Shin-Buddhism.

In august of 2001, I met Basilio, my son's biological father and once again found myself pregnant early into the relationship. I am totally against abortions, so I strongly and willingly tried to make things work considering the circumstances. On October 8 of 2002, I gave birth to a six-pound baby boy. Unfortunately, the relationship only lasted for a short time due to his numerous counts of infidelity and the mental and physical abuse he inflicted upon me. I can't even begin to describe the kind of abuse I endured, for that could be another book of its own.

By April of 2003, I was a single mom again, now with two children. I had to wise up quickly because I was not about to recklessly commit myself to another unhealthy and or abusive relationship, never mind bare another child out of wedlock. I made the decision to further my education because I was the only financial resource for my children and knew that a higher income was needed if we were going to live somewhat comfortably. For me, getting a higher education seemed to be the only option. I always worked full-time, no matter the circumstances, and with much endurance and commitment, I obtained a bachelor's degree in healthcare sciences. I even ended up on the dean's list two years in a row throughout my toughest semesters.

It would be the first time in my life that I would finally start feeling proud and confident of myself and my achievements. I thrived on intelligence and constant learning, which helped to drive my continuous will power, especially during times of doubt and uncertainty. I was finally gaining intellectual strength, which seemed to help relieve my burdened feelings of unworthiness that originated from early childhood. On the flip side, this caused a bit of a set back with my faith.

By 2006, I had not only obtained a bachelor's degree, but also an associate's degree in legal studies and criminology. It was during this time in my life that I grew close to a co-worker who was a Christian. We had much in common and I was thrilled to start attending Sunday services again, because in my heart, I always longed for the Lord's presence. The congregation was called "Church of Christ" and I was supremely excited to be given the opportunity to feel the presence of God in my life once again, and this time, I was determined to stay and not flee my responsibility as a servant of God. I honestly concede that throughout my many experiences of reverence, Christianity in particular, always felt the most clean and pure within its forms of worship. In contrast, my accumulations of past mistakes, fears and regrets was once again starting to resurface psychologically. Nonetheless, I was adamant to rekindle my relationship with the Lord by going to church again, even if I couldn't make it every Sunday. During this time church felt different in a positive way, and like never before, I really enjoyed getting to know the church and its members. In addition, the environment in this particular parish always felt nurturing and genuine.

As we all know, friendships can come and go, and once again, another friendship gracefully faded. Although we occasionally kept in touch, by the end of 2007, our lasting friendship came to a halt. In spite of this, I did still attend a few more Sunday services at her church, but only if she invited me to go. Once it started getting really uncomfortable to continue my association, my kids and I quit going altogether, but my faith in God strongly sustained. Ironically, I never seemed to be able to commit myself to any one church and I never understood why. Maybe I was meant to experience the different cultures and the occults in preparation of recognizing the true faith that would eventually come down the pipeline.

As I progressively continued to mature, unfortunately some friendships did not. While some relationships faded back and forth in my life, a few stayed consistently throughout, including my friend Jennifer. I met Jennifer when we were both in our teens, at fourteen years of age to be exact. It was a turbulent relationship from the start as we were both very hard headed and quick tempered, but one thing always kept us in common; we were both victims of sexual abuse by the hands of trusted men. I was very clingy towards her and her friendship in the beginning as I was constantly trying to seek her company. She was quite striking with her appearance and never had problems with gaining the attention of men. I'm not sure if she was raised catholic, but I believe probably so, for she would only attend services at "Saint Mary's Catholic Cathedral." In her early twenties, she also became a single mom and left an abusive relationship due to very similar circumstances like mine. We always had a common understanding and counseled each other quite often.

As the friendship weaned back and forth, by our mid to late twenties, I observed her commitment to the Lord as she attended mass on Sundays. I would join her on numerous occasions, but I noticed that the experience sometimes left me feeling culpable and disgraced. This made absolutely no sense and I pondered on this question for quite some time. Was it possible for true worshipers who tried living righteously to feel cumbersome in the house of God? I always felt the uneasiness but, thankfully our Lord is patient and kind and was willing to wait for my acceptance.

The on and off attachment ultimately came to an end due to a quarrel over a love interest, and by the time I turned 30 years old, it was totally over. She tried to reach out to me several times, but I never returned her calls. This was her ultimate betrayal, and I had no intention of ever reconnecting with her again. It was also around this time when I met Todd, who is now my husband. It was a blessing to finally be able to meet a decent guy who only wasn't a liar and a cheater but a person that would ultimately accept my kids as his own.

The year 2014 was pretty intense and although I was now in a very committed relationship, I was still desperate for answers in my life and where it was going. While out shopping one day, I bumped into an old colleague of mine whom I use to work with years ago. We ended up exchanging phone numbers and naturally, instantly became friends again. She was having marital problems with her husband at the time which caused her to regularly seek psychic readings, which seemed to be her only option for answers at the time. The more we hung out, the closer we grew in our pits of despair, for I obviously had resolving issues myself. Within a matter of a few months, she eventually convinced me to get a tarot card reading for myself and since I was already in the habit of reading my daily horoscope anyway, I thought, *Why not?* Plus, the psychic was willing to give us a discount referral because my friend was a regular returning client of hers. I remember driving over an hour for the appointment just to meet her. The reading was to take place in a small spiritual business store, and although I can no longer recall the location, I do vividly remember the inside appearance.

Like most spiritual boutiques, the aroma of patchouli was quite overwhelming. My first observation upon entering the store was the numerous amounts of black raven taxidermy scattered throughout the shop's book shelves. The shop was quite small and so I noticed the large wall tapestry in the back of the store immediately. The fabric appeared to sparkle with glitter and the beautiful fairy that was embroider on the canvas appeared to be fluttering its wings. To the left of the tapestry was a door with a room where the reading was going to take place.

The atmosphere felt very magical, as if I had just entered into another space and time. As I looked through their selection of books while waiting for the psychic to arrive, I became very aware of the shop's indications and practices towards Wicca, witchcraft and sorcery. It was creepy and exciting at the same time. The owner of the store seemed to take a liking to me right away and tried to maintain my constant attention by showing me her selections of jewelry, crystals, spell books, candles and lotions and potions. She had a Bohemian style appearance with beautifully long red hair. I admit, she was very alluring and carried herself with much charisma. I was restricted with my spending and didn't have much money, and so I declined all her offerings.

Finally, the time came and the psychic reader arrived. Her gait seemed to waddle and her body composure was undeniably frail. She had whitish gray hair, and if I was to guess, I think she was probably in her sixties.

She didn't seem intimidating at first, and as she asked me to have a seat, I thought to myself, *there is no harm in this*. Right away, she asked me for my date of birth and my full first and last name. She also asked me to physically write down my questions on a piece of white paper. The first ten minutes of the reading seemed routine and somewhat stagnant.

In the beginning of the reading I couldn't relate to anything or anybody that she was bringing through, and I remember thinking; *This lady is a complete fake!*

That is until the moment she suddenly stopped playing with her tarot cards and looked at me straight in the eyes with a threatening like demeanor and said the following: *"I need to inform you of something important, and the message is urgent and is coming forth now."*

She told me that, like her, I also had a special gift and that I've had the endowment since early childhood. Although I already knew this about myself, it was still frightening to hear. She further continued to tell me that I was very lucky to have such gifts, and that my angels and spirit guides were now urging me to give way.

In that very moment, the background noises in the shop room slowly started muffling out, and for a second, I paused in fear and utter silence. I sensed a sudden heaviness in the air and as my gaze locked on her eyes and lips, I felt like I was being hypnotized. She continued on and said; *"There is also a male figure spirit energy with you who is about thirty-two years of age and he knows you from another life."*

She further said, *"I believe this specific male spirit is a lifetime partner and has been watching over you for quite some time now"*.

Then she asked if I knew who this person was with curiosity and an oddly nervous hesitation. I honestly had no idea of whom she was talking about and she went on to say, *"My dear, your spirit guides consist mostly of male energies and they have been waiting for you to seek them out since you were born."*

It became apparent that I was being recruited to do psychic work, and by the end of the reading she convinced me that it was my duty to do so. She whispered in a seductive manner and said, *"My child, this is your destiny calling and a gift that is unknown to others."* She finished by saying, *"I see that you are a healer and see many people flocking to you for assistance in the near future."*

Not knowing what I know now, I remained glued to the chair as she continued interviewing me. I remember feeling suddenly faint in my disposition and wanted to know who the spirit was that told her about my clairvoyance and paranormal occurrences because I feared it was the very same demon that had taunted me for so many years.

My palms became drenched with sweat and I felt like I was going to have a severe panic attack at that moment. As the reading continued flashes of my childhood experiences with the taunting spirit arose, for it was now confirmed that my encounters with the apparition world wasn't just a figment of my imagination and or a hallucination but rather a true reality.

I never shared those frightening experiences with anyone but yet she seemed to know. As the reading was ending, I become immensely frightened and ended the session abruptly. I didn't know at the time that God was trying to warn me to stop and signaling danger throughout the entire reading.

The fear that God was trying to instill in me in those moments was not out of demand but rather love.

I believe God was telling me, *"Hey you're playing with fire, and you will surely get burned."*

I remember pacing back and forth and feeling anxious to leave as I waited for my friend to finish with her reading. The ride home seemed to painstakingly take forever that day and while I was shaken with fear, my friend on the other hand was ecstatic. Obviously, this experience affected me tremendously and I began to play with the idea of doing personal psychic readings.

Not before long, it quickly escalated into an obsession and I started to constantly watch television shows based on psychic detective work, hauntings and anything that was on the subject of paranormal phenomena.

By the end of 2015, my staggering collection of books based on numerology, astrology, palm reading, tarot reading, clairvoyance, book of dreams, contacting your spirit guide and holistic energy healing ballooned out of control. My entire bookcase, which was in the dining room at the time, became infused with books based on new age and mysticism. The authors included Sylvia Brown, Doreen Virtue, James Van Praagh and John Edward to name a few.

Before I knew it, I was hooked, and without realizing, I temporarily lost sight of God and his existence. On a side note, I always made sure to keep my kids out of all this and at all times practiced my spiritualism in private as best as I could. Todd on the other hand seemed to ignore my fruition and just kind of rolled with the punches. He has always supported my new endeavors but also let me have my personal space, therefore, he never showed much interest in the details of my psychic readings.

On November 16, 2015, a supernatural incident occurred that I feel is extremely paramount to share in this story. This encounter became a pivotal turning point in my life because it ultimately ended up influencing my decision-making process with aspects to pursuing my psychic/medium work. I knew my experiences were real but this time the spirit stepped it up a notch by displaying its intelligence during daylight and in public. It also provided me with irrevocable evidence of the existence of invisible forces, which I would eventually come to learn, is a type of ominous trickery that is used by demons in hopes of luring the searching soul.

Sure enough, the tactic worked and I took the bait. It was my scheduled day off from work and I decided to take a quick trip to my favorite bookstore (Barnes and Noble) with the anticipation of finding another new book to read.

Once again, I found myself in the new age books section. As I stood there with a blank stare not knowing which book to pick, all of a sudden, this random book gently propelled itself from the top shelf and landed on my feet.

As I bent over to quickly pick it up, I franticly looked around my surroundings in search of others in hopes that someone else witnessed what just had happened. It was surreal, as if the spirit world was now determined to make their presence known, not only in the public but during daytime hours. This was huge, and in a nonsensical way, flattering and alluring because subconsciously, there was an underlying seduction behind the scheme.

The book was called "The Reluctant Psychic" written by Suzan Saxman. By this time, I was remarkably lost in true faith and falsely forced myself to accept this occurrence as a sign.

I purchased the book right away and as soon as I got home, I dove right into reading. Right from the start I could not put the book down because the author's story seemed to resonate intensely with mine. I finished the book in less than a week which prompted me to make the decision to come out of hiding with my psychic abilities. I had finally given into what I believed was a life calling and totally surrendered myself to the world of fortune telling and mysticism. I felt invigorated, as if a big burden has been lifted off my shoulders and I could be who I was meant to be all along. Or so I thought.

CHAPTER 4:
MY LIFE AS A PSYCHIC MEDIUM

There shall not be found among you anyone who makes his son or his daughter pass through the fire, one who uses divination, one who practices witchcraft, or one who interprets omens, or a sorcerer, or one who casts a spell, or a medium, or a spiritist, or one who calls up the dead. For whoever does these things is detestable to the Lord.
(Deuteronomy 18:10)

By January of 2016, my new mission in life became apparent and my spiritual lifestyle evident as I now openly practiced as a successful psychic medium. As selfish as it sounds, I loved being in demand and as my popularity increased with other psychic mediums I finally felt like I belonged. I was swept away by the power that came with this line of work and became fully addicted. At times, I would catch myself seeking that sort of attention for not so good reasons.

To the contrary, I was humbled to know that I was helping, healing and changing people's lives for the better. I was not only inspired but deeply moved by the multitude of transformations that took place right before my eyes. I can only describe the experiences as indescribably beautiful.

As we all know, there are many other competing psychic/mediums out there ready to serve the lost whom are looking for answers and for this reason I felt compelled to excel my skills in order to become the best of the best.

Now that I think about it, I wanted to stand out and prove my worthiness out of envy and natural competitiveness. I ended up enrolling myself in various local classes, workshops, web-seminars and attended numerous psychic fairs. I even took a tarot card reading class, and although I was never attracted to do readings in that form, I was willing to learn all the ins and outs of the occult.

To me it was pertinent to get an understanding of the legalities of the business and these classes provided the specifics. The tuition fees were absolutely ridiculous, and prices varied from as low as $250 to as high as $3,000, depending on the course level you were trying to achieve. I couldn't believe the massive amounts of selections of programs that were readily available out there with just a click of a button. Some institutes even offered payment plans for applicants who were experiencing financial hardship. I will not expose the sources because my goal is not to slander but to educate the reader.

By early July 2016, I had completed six to eight classes of courses in psyche learning and had acquired multiple certificates throughout the process. It was solely for authentication purposes because although I knew of my gift, I still needed direction of how to use it properly and professionally. That piece of paper with the gold stamp made me feel validated and I was ready to start my own business. It was now becoming very obvious of just how deeply consumed I had become with seeking that constant communication from the spirit world and as a result I started becoming immensely withdrawn from the outside world. I didn't realize just yet of how isolated and obsessed I had become with the cult, but it's exactly what the devil wanted, my entire being all to himself. My husband even noticed the startling change in my behavior and attitude and grew quite concerned with it.

Besides the readings, I was also generously offering reiki energy and crystal healing sessions during my house calls, and my clients absolutely loved it. Sometimes I would even be referenced and compared as "the shaman healer". I have heard the term shaman before but only in the native American culture, thus far, it was very flattering. Often the sessions would end up turning into a psychic reading because I was especially clairvoyant under such intimate circumstances and felt obligated to share the visions and insights that would present themselves to me. I can't count how many times the spirit world would flash an opened third eye during my reiki sessions. The huge eye ball would move back and forth, side to side, in a three-dimensional projection, like something out of a horror movie. The spirit world is clever and has the absolute power to allure the human spirit by any means necessary in an attempt to trap you further into their mystical realm.

I always knew when I was about to receive telepathic information. The signals and supernatural communication always got my attention and would usually occur in the same following manner.

- **First**: A loud frequency with vibrational buzzing in the right ear, which would usually occur between midnight and three a.m.

- **Second**: Flashes of white light followed by a multitude of visions.

- **Third:** Muffled voices coming in an out; Once the voices became clear I would begin to receive random messages, followed by an influx of pertinent information; Mostly about people, places and things.

Trust me when I say this, it is all for the wrong reasons and their intentions are nothing short of pure evil. Their purpose is solely evident, which is to give you supernatural powers in exchange for your soul at the time of death. The more hypnotized I became, the stronger the devil was able to tighten his deathly grip on me, and this time he wasn't going let me go without a fight, which I would later discover on my journey into darkness.

In September of 2016, I decided to take my work to the extreme and joined a paranormal investigation group that was located in the southeast part of Connecticut. They were in need of a medium for their investigations, and they accepted my application immediately. There is a direct purpose to this part in my story, and that is to once again expose the existence of the invisible world and the evil forces behind the veil.

In was the month of October and the team and I were scheduled to meet at an old art theater building which stood secluded on a college campus. We were scheduled to meet at 10:00 p.m. I arrived thirty minutes early and waited anxiously to start.

It was a chilly Friday night and I still recall how my eyes watered immensely from the cold windy chill while walking across the parking lot. The scheduled investigation was to start at approximately 11:00 p.m. and was estimated to finish around 2:00 a.m. the following morning.

As I waited for everyone to arrive, something didn't feel right, and although I had a bit of a nauseating feeling, I pushed myself to stay anyway.

The equipment set up took hours, and the investigation didn't start until after midnight. There were numerous different metaphysical gadgets that we were going to use, and the ghost box was one of them. This device is designed to pick up voices from potential entities that we cannot see with the naked eye.

The team split into three different sections of the theater, and I ended up being stationed with four other team members on the third floor where the theater was located, directly across from the stage in the tower pit. We were instructed to try to pick up activity with the ghost box and was forwardly encouraged to provoke the unseen.

As the four of us were sitting there in the pitch dark, the ghost box started making static noises, almost like a radio station that couldn't tune in. There was a pause of silence, then all of the sudden, a deep growled male voice started emitting through the ghost box speaker and in a demanding manner called my name. There was no mistake; he definitely said my name loud and clear!

I let out a small giggle out of pure fear and outwardly asked, "What the hell was that?"

Then the entity said my name again!

As one could imagine, this would be a resolutely startling encounter for a lot of people, including myself. The crew in the room must have been amused because one of the paranormal investigators turned to me and said maliciously, I guess they must like you, and started laughing.

This intense feeling of horror took over me and I wanted nothing more but to run for my life. I appeared calm and collective physically but, in the inside, I was screaming for help. I feared that I would be made fun of and thought of as an amateur and so I forced myself to stay throughout the entire investigation.

Later that morning we decided to investigate the rehearsal room located on the first floor. It was pitch dark and as soon as the door closed behind me, I knew something was wrong.

There were three of us in the room, all females, including myself. I should have known better not to try to conjure evil spirits, but at the time that is not the way I perceived it to be. The goosebumps that I experienced felt unusually different and seemed to resemble the feelings of an intense sting followed by a painful burning sensation as if I was being attacked with small tiny poking needles.

It was quiet for about ten minutes and as I sat there in the darkness trying to hear any sound, I remember thinking to myself that this was something I should not be doing.

Suddenly I felt something tugging on the back of my pants. I let out a little scream and told the girls to cut it out and quit playing around.

One of the team members said, "what are you talking about?" We're on the other side of the room, nowhere near you."

A silent awkwardness filled the room and a few minutes later the tug happened again. I panicked and demanded the light to be turned on immediately. Once the lights came back on, I noticed that the girls were being honest and that they were standing at least ten feet away from me. I pretended to be calm but internally I was freaking out.

I couldn't wait to get home that morning and remember feeling exceptionally frightened about it all. I was completely creeped out and although I wanted to continue my psychic work, this event scared the living daylights out of me and I never made contact with the group again.

That day I promised myself to stick with the basics of mediumship work, however the devil thought otherwise as he continuously kept stringing me along. The signs were all there that this was trouble yet I continued to pursue the unseen.

One of the many rooms where I performed readings for clients and students.

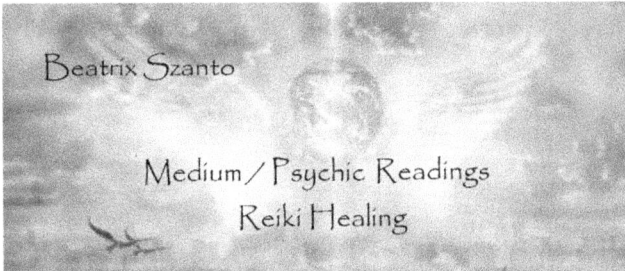

Beatrix Szanto

Medium / Psychic Readings
Reiki Healing

My first business card 2016.

5-star Reviews from previous clients from my past life as a psychic/medium

Home   Posts   Reviews   Videos   Photos

⚙ Options

~~1 year ago~~

5 stars

Beatrix is by far one of my favorite holistic practitioners. Although the work she performs is nothing short of a miracle, her down-to-earth spirit and kind heart makes it feel like you're sitting down for a simple conversation with an old friend. What sets Beatrix apart from the rest is her drive to deliver the highest quality readings with the most accuracy possible. I'm constantly amazed by the tiny nuances she picks up on when communicating with my loved ones and the respect she shows the spirits she works with. Beatrix is definitely my go-to person when I need to make connections with loved ones who have passed.

👍 Like   💬 Comment   ↪ Share

1 year ago · 🌐

5 stars

Bea is awesome enjoyed my reading think she is spot on ... amazing!!

❤ Beatrix Szanto

👍 Like   💬 Comment   ↪ Share

Home   Posts   Reviews   Videos   Photos   At

⚙ Options

1 year ago · 🌐

5 stars

Was told of Beatrix through a friend. I reached out to her and received a responded same day, very informative and sincere. My first experience connecting with a loved one that has passed. Beatrix knew nothing of me or of my grandfather and her description of my grandfather was exact. I was so overwhelmed with emotion I could not stop crying. To be able to connect with my grandfather gave me an opportunity to ask him many questions and be able to get answers, which I needed so very much. I was able to apologize and know that he knows that I had no choice. Being able to connect with my grandfather provided me with the motivation to handle the family matters better. I will do all I can to do as my grandfather ask and it is possible thanks to Beatrix. I will be scheduling another session. Thank you

🔘 Beatrix Szanto

👍 Like   💬 Comment   ↗ Share

1 year ago · 🌐

5 stars

Beatrix has an amazing gift, she is genuine, confident, easy to talk to..
On my second reading she helped me connect with a loved one who had passed 10 years ago. What an experience, I am short of words... Truly a joyous experience.
Thank you for your time and dedication.

⊙ Beatrix Szanto

👍 Like   💬 Comment   ➣ Share

1 year ago · 🌐

5 stars

Just had a reading with Beatrix .Shes the best made me feel completely at ease. Seemed to know me even tho we had never met before .She has much insight into the people who have passed names things that have happened. I would definitely recommend her to all my friends.THANKS. AGAIN BEATRIX◆

👍❤ 2   1 Comment

👍 Like   💬 Comment   ➣ Share

CHAPTER 5:
SUPERNATURAL MANIFESTATION

The Manifestation on the Index Card.

This picture above was originally a plain blank white index card before the imprint manifestation. This supernatural occurrence took place in March of 2017 during the midst of my spiritualistic practices.

Today, I carry this proof of evidence around with me everywhere, just in case I come across a non-believer in the near future.

I eventually had this laminated so the colors will sustain and to prevent fading. I would later discover that this ink photo is of the famous Saint Peter during whom appeared shaken at the time when Jesus was carrying his cross to be crucified. I did not pay much attention to this at first because I was use to paranormal experiences as such, although not to this extent. This authentic piece of artifact stays close to my heart and is proof that Saint Peter was protecting me long before my fall as a psychic/medium.

CHAPTER 6:
DECEPTION UNVEILED

Beloved, do not believe every spirit, but test the spirits to see whether they are from God, for many false prophets have gone out into the world.
(1 John 4:1)

In late spring of 2017, I decided to turn my psychic work in a different direction. Whether it was out of curiosity or just plain boredom, I will never know, but either way things were about to take a huge turn in my life.

My new focus came about when another psychic friend of mine asked me to help her with an unsolved murder case that took place twenty years ago. Honestly, I am not even sure if she even asked for the help, maybe she was just looking for a much needed second opinion, but either way, I jumped right in.

I knew my psychic friend well, for she had also taken some of the same psychic courses with me earlier. She had seen my work before and trusted me enough to seek my assistance. Prior to this, we use to practice doing readings on each other in class for fun and I always felt supported by her. She had the look of mysticism written all over her, plus she had a comedic side to her, which was hard to resist.

I remember the day like it was yesterday, when she first texted me about the case. I had just gotten home from work and was exhausted from the day. I was still in my work scrubs as I started cooking dinner, and as I was standing over the hot stove, my phone notified me of an incoming text.

The sound of the notification seemed louder than usual which caused me to instantly look at my phone in a nervous manner. At first, she didn't give me any detailed information about the case, but by the end of the night I was able to narrow down both of the killer's physical features, possible locations, and characteristics of the perpetrators. It was exciting to think that we could possibly crack open an old unsolved murder case, and I couldn't have been more thrilled at the time as it seemed we were about to embark on a new journey and rescue mission and possibly play a psychic detective role. It was at this time that things took a different turn, and not exactly for the better.

As we progressed with the case, I noticed that I seemed to be the only one that was being used as conduit, because most of the time the information was only being transmitted through me.

The sessions would always take place in the wee hours of the night, specifically after 1:00 a.m. in the morning. I call them "sessions" because during the encounters, I would always write the information down either on my phone or on a piece of paper. The intelligence would communicate a multitude of information, including the mental traits and the unique features of both the murderers. For instance, one of the killers involved had acne pock scars on his face and wore thick coke bottled glasses. Spirit got specific and even gave nicknames of the people involved including their gang affiliation and their specific cult symbol.

I now knew the significance of the red balloons that I was constantly being shown and the RV that the victim's parents used to take family trips with including the dog that sat in the front of the RV. The evil spirit also made sure never to miss a session either, no matter what the circumstances were, even if I was to the extreme point of exhaustion. My psychic partner in crime was now becoming seemingly perplexed with aspects to the immense amount of accurate information I was constantly giving her.

I am sure she grew a little annoyed with me since I was constantly blowing up her phone in the middle of the night with my never-ending texting. She lived an hour away and phone texting became our main form of communication.

I was constantly writing stuff down too, and at one given point I even sketched a picture of the bridge including its surrounding area where I envisioned the killer disposing his car.

It became obvious that we needed to have a weekend meet just to be able to compare notes and to create a collage case file, just like the other professional detectives would do. Eventually I did end up taking that weekend trip up to her house, which I believe caused a chain reaction of events that ultimately led me to the painful realization that

I was in very deep trouble with the spirit world and its malevolent forces.

On July 28, I reported to my usual work shift. I was exhausted from the night before because once again I was up all night communicating with my so-called spirit guides.

At first, I always welcomed the information, but now it was starting to become intrusive as the flow of communication became constant, even during daylight. Still I contemplated back and forth throughout that morning of whether or not I should report my findings to law enforcement, but was very reluctant to do so because of the nature of the case and the people involved. Police have been known to work with psychics before, but I also knew that the chances of them taking me seriously was slim to none. Or was it?

I felt restless and uneasy as the day progressed. Around 11:35 a.m. I made the random decision to cut my work day short and asked my boss if I could leave early. I had this uncontrollable feeling of wanting to leave work and I couldn't wait to get out the door fast enough. As I rushed to grab my purse, all of a sudden, this overwhelming feeling of nausea started to overcome my state of well-being.

I became jittery and my head felt like it was going to explode, all within a period of a few minutes. I left with the intention of going straight home and quickly got into my truck and started driving directly towards my usual route, which was the highway, except this time I never made it to the on ramp.

Abruptly, without thinking, I decided to turn on the opposite direction of the highway, which was route 91 north, rather than my usual south direction. I was now heading towards the home town of where the murder took place.

I honestly don't recall how this all came about, but the next thing I know, I am walking barefoot throughout a wooded area, desperately trying to get to a specific area by a body of water under a bridge that was located near a set of train tracks. The scene and layout of the area was quite creepy and for a moment I felt like I was mad woman with a vengeance.

As I slipped in and out of my worldly existence, I was finally able to snap out of my science fiction experience and once I came to my senses I was absolutely shocked with the realization of where I was and what had just occurred.

The time was now 4:15 p.m. and I had no clue as to how I just lost over three hours of my existence into the twilight zone. I frantically reached out to my psychic friend and after informing her of my crazy situation she grew concerned, mostly because I was not only alone but far from home. I could tell that she was genuinely concerned but I really don't think she knew what to say, probably because she knew the seriousness of the situation and didn't know what to make of it. She offered to stay on the phone with me until I made it safely to my vehicle, but I declined.

Fear was now setting in and as I frantically tried to make my way back to the truck it became evident that I was in a place that looked exactly like the visionary drawing I previously drew. I will never forget the view and the intense smell of raw sewage that filled heavy in the air.

The landscape was filled with old trash, discarded furniture, mattresses and rusted car parts, resembling a scene much like the ones that they use in rated-R movies.

I didn't get any sleep that night and the following morning I decided that it was time for me to take a break from psychic work. However, the spirit wasn't going to give me that break and I was now no longer able to control my third eye's on and off switch.

It was at this time that my husband really took a notice to the major change in my behavior and expressed his concern with an angry outburst that would cause me to give him the silent treatment for the next couple of days.

What I learned the hard way is that what demons did and could do in the Bible times, they can still very much do today. Their insinuations are deceptive, manipulative, seductive and alluring.

People tend to easily fall for the fascination of an exhilarating new message or its messenger, and unfortunately, end up susceptible to the deception out of desperation.

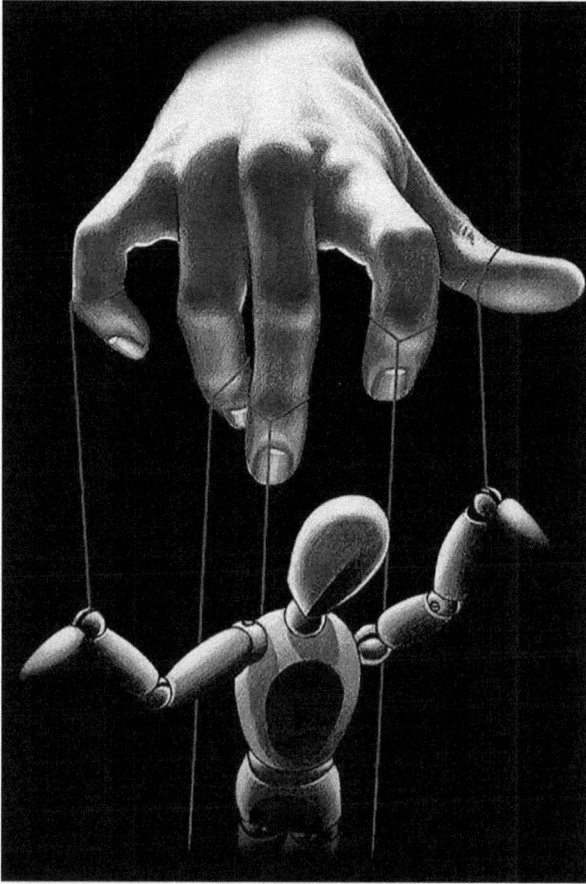

"Now the spirit clearly says that in later times some will abandon the faith and follow deceiving spirits and things taught by demons" (1 Timothy 4:1)

My vision of Hell.

CHAPTER 7:
A GLIMPSE OF HELL

One night after about a week after my unsettling experience, I abruptly awoke around 2:30 a.m. I sat up in an attempt to walk to the bathroom but for someone reason I felt too frightened to make a move and this stopped me dead in my tracks. Unexpectedly something drew my attention over to the right side of my room where the old brick wall divider stood and what I saw next looked like something out of a sci-fi horror movie. A female entity with long black hair, who appeared to be demon possessed was slowly crawling its way towards me on the hardwood floor. The demon looked like the main character out of a movie called "The Ring." I suddenly felt paralyzed and couldn't feel my arms or legs. What I encountered next gave me the confirmation and the warning that hell does in fact exist and that if I continued to practice magic, that is exactly where I would end up. The visual scenario projected into my state of consciousness during my subdued paralyzed state went as follows:

Without much warning, except for the evil entity that was crawling on my bedroom floor, I was placed in an enclosed cave like chamber which appeared to resemble a dungeon from the medieval era. There was an opened hatch which led to a gothic appearing hallway. It was very dim and the only reason I was able to see is because there were torch lights attached to the dungeon's walls. I started to float down the hall and at this point I knew that I was now in spirit form rather than in my earthbound body. I took an immediate notice to the rotten stench of death and the moldy wetness that seemed to encompass the walls of this underground pit. Looking down I noticed a stairway that appeared to spiral down into a deep dark black hole. Then suddenly, above the stairway, a twisted and disfigured looking demon appeared and was now making its way towards me. It was crawling on the ceiling walls like a spider and its head was extremely twisted and cocked sideways.

This appalling figure was staring me down like I was about to be his dinner for the night and I knew that if I went any further, I would enter into a dwelling place of pure evil. I then heard screaming, crying and painful moans and groans that I can't even begin to describe. I thought to myself, my God, this must be the entrance to hell and it does exist. I then heard a voice say "This is a place of desecration." I didn't even know what that word meant at the time, besides all I wanted to do was awake and break free from the evil suppression I was experiencing. I remember finally feeling alert and conscious but I still couldn't open my eyes. I struggled to open my eyelids, which seemed like an eternity, but once I finally did, I went into a state of pure dread.

I wanted to wake my husband up but I felt too weak to try. I forcefully prompted myself up into an upward sitting position and once I felt strong enough to stand, I walked over to the corner of the room where my alter and shrine prayer stood. The stand had many figurines, crystals, sage grass, and native American feathers on it. I lit up the candle that hung beneath my guardian angel statue and quickly fell to my knees and started praying specifically to the Archangel Michael. I happened to study angelology and knew that Archangel Michael was at the top of the hierarchy of angels and that he was considered to be in charge as far as protecting human souls within the earth's angelic realm.

I should have prayed to God, but I felt ashamed and too far gone with my unique situation by this time. Besides, in new age and mysticism, we are taught to pray to the universal forces, angels, spirit guides and or idols, like Ganesh or Buddha. I couldn't get the smell of stench out of my nose and the odor I smelled during my vision. I now understood that an evil spiritual force was attached to me and my home. It was at this time that I became painstakingly aware of the fact that I needed to reach out to a professional, or at least to a person who would have knowledge of what steps to take in order to successfully rid evil omens and or spirits. Although I constantly used sage to cleanse my home with sweet grasses, there was never any proof that the process actually worked.

A friend of mine who was more seasoned in this type of work recommended that I reach out to an old teacher of hers who was a well-known shaman teacher and healer. It was on a Sunday that I ultimately ended up reaching out to her through e-mail with a detailed explanation of my situation. As I anxiously waited for a response, I suddenly started feeling ill with symptoms of nausea, lethargy, and dizziness. I thought maybe I was having a hypoglycemic attack since I had not eaten anything most of the day. I stayed in bed all day Monday, July 30th and finally got the response I've been waiting for the following morning, Tuesday, July 31st.

I remember the day clearly, for it was the day the bomb of truth exploded in my face, which to this day I still consider the scariest day of my life. It was the day of a sheer and stark truth, a day when the devil's deception slowly started to unveil. The shaman healer urged me to seek an exorcism, and sooner rather than later. She further told me that the only group of people she knew that could do these kinds of cleansings was located out of South America by the Amazon River. This obviously wasn't possible to carry out and I felt desperate and clueless with what to do next.

I remember reading her email at least ten times or so, because I could not believe or comprehend what I was reading. Still laying ill in bed with much weakness upon me, I laid there frozen and paralyzed as the stream of tears were now rolling down my face. It was day three of feeling spiritually sick; I still had no appetite and or strength to even get out of bed. The continuous sheer visions that the demons were now inflicting upon me was nothing short of psychological torture. Anytime I tried to close my eyes, the enemy would flash frightening images in my field of vision, in an attempt to subdue my soul and prevent escape by intimidating me with fear. I know that the last person I should have reached out to was a shaman, but considering the facts, I felt that nobody else would understand my circumstance.

Shamans are considered medicine priest or priestess of the spirit world who uses magic for good and or bad purposes, and although they are considered dangerous, I still believe that God used her for his purpose as an informant to convey the critical message that would ultimately save my life. Reality hit hard, and because I knew the truth of my circumstance, I felt utterly defeated and totally betrayed.

CHAPTER 8:
EXORCISM

As we were going to the place of prayer, we were met by a slave girl who had a spirit of divination and brought her owners much gain by fortune-telling. She followed Paul and us, crying out, "These men are the servants of the most high God, who proclaim to you the way of salvation" and this she kept doing for many days. Paul, having become greatly annoyed, turned and said to the spirit, "I command you in the name of Jesus Christ to come out of her." And it came out that very hour.
(Acts 16:16-18)

Days later I was still feeling physically and mentally ill and as my despair set in, I slowly mustered up the strength to get out of bed and put some clothes on in order to try to get some fresh air. I wanted to call my husband at work to admit my situation but something held me back. I was frightened, embarrassed and worried that he wouldn't understand of what was happening. I mean stuff like this only happens in the movies. I slowly made my way down the stairs and as I headed towards the kitchen sink to get some water, suddenly this ominous evil voice echoed in my ear and said the following:

"Bitch, why don't you go and kill yourself or I'll do it for you".

Out of utter terror I dropped my cup on the floor and frantically ran outside to my back yard.

Once I made it to a grassy area on the hill that was located in the back of the house, I suddenly fell to my knees in an involuntarily manner. It was as if somebody or something drop kicked my legs so I couldn't run away. Like a crazy lady I started to loudly command the spirit to leave my body and my home. I don't know what gave me the idea but somehow, I knew that I needed to confront the demon that was attacking me. I repeated the command over and over again, no less than a hundred times.

I could barely support my body's weight and as my wrists gave in, I ended up falling down then rolling on my back. As I stared into the beautiful sky and its large white clouds, I yelled out, "What in the world have I done! What have I done!" My head was pounding and I noticed that my neck and head was mildly trembling back and forth without my control. I felt like I was going to vomit and slightly started choking on my own spit. It took a tremendous amount of strength to be able to pull myself up and once I was able to stand, I wobbled over to my patio swing and sat down so I could catch my breath. As I tried to gather my thoughts together, one thing was imminent, I was in desperate need of God's intervention and I needed to find help without delay.

Out of a craze, I stood up and ran back in the house to grab my keys and jumped in my car with one purpose in mind, which was, to find a catholic church with a priest that could perform either a healing or a full-blown exorcism. I attempted to call my husband once again and this time I was determined to come clean, even if it meant losing his support. I didn't get specific about my situation over the phone, I just told him to come home as soon as possible because there was something very wrong and if he didn't, I was going to call 911 for help. He was very comforting and I recognized the concern in his voice as he assured me that he would be home in less than one hour. I started to panic again with the fear that my son would come home from school just in time only to witness a frightening scene that would traumatize him forever.

All I could think about was my son's and daughter's future and the horrible things that would happen if I left my existence that day. Who would raise my son? Although my husband and I have been living together for the past ten years, I wasn't sure if he would take that task on. My daughter was now independent and living with her boyfriend but we still had a close mother and daughter relationship and she would have been deeply affected by the loss. She knew of my gift but never really took full interest in the matter. Sitting in despair and thinking about the loss of my family ultimately gave me the extra boost of strength that I needed to continue to fight whatever was coming my way and to act quickly.

It was now around noon and I was driving around like a crazy woman looking for a church in town in hopes that at least one of them would be open for service. After driving around for an hour with no luck, this feeling of impending doom suddenly overcame me and once again I started feeling ill. I knew that I needed to get back home quickly so I could lay back down in order to get grips of myself and avoid a hospitalization. Either way, I knew that if I called emergency services and explained my circumstance they would laugh and think that I was on drugs and hallucinating, which definitely was not the case. I pulled in my driveway and got a strong urge to look up at my bedroom windows because I knew that something was up there. The last thing anyone would want to do including myself is to go back inside and face the spiritual warfare. I opened the door, carefully walked in and picked up the broken cup that I dropped on the floor earlier.

I took another cup and forced myself to take in couple of sips of water; subsequently it was day two of having no fluids, and if it wasn't for the side rails in the stair hallway, I would of never have been able to drag myself back upstairs to bed. It was at this time when my husband pulled up in the driveway and quickly came to my aid upstairs. I confessed my truth and fear but not to the full extent and surprisingly he didn't seem surprised by my situation. He explained that he had suspicions due to the weirdness of my behavior and was very glad that I no longer wanted anything to do with psychic/medium work. He recommended that I get some rest and didn't comprehend the danger at hand because I didn't get into the full details of my ordeal. I preferred to keep it that way in any case because I knew that if he knew the specifics of my warfare it would frighten him to the point where he would have wanted nothing to do with me.

No sooner than I lay down, the verbal attack started again and this time I was being called every name in the book. I can't even bring myself to repeat the language that was used, but I can tell you that the word *"cunt"* was prominent among the many. Not being able to bare another minute of this entity's presence I turned on my collection of relaxing music in an attempt to block everything out. As weak as I was, I was still able to reach over to my nightstand and push the play button on my iPhone. I started to drift off into a mild transient state of sleep but was abruptly woken by a very disturbing vision. A vision, that I now know, was sent to confirm my suspicion of a possession. A vision that not only helped but ultimately propelled me to seek help immediately that day.

The scene was live and in color as if it was happening right before my eyes. I observed my cat (Kabbalah) squirming on the floor trying to regurgitate and vomit in an aggressive fashion. I could even hear the loud noises of her gagging as she was evidently struggling to spit something up but to no avail.

Once I became fully awake, a soft vibrating voice whispered, *"Jacobs Ladder"*. It was now around two o'clock in the afternoon, and the spiritual warfare was in full affect. I picked up my cell phone and google searched the words Jacob's Ladder so I could figure out what the message meant. Of course, the first thing that popped up was the movie called Jacobs Ladder, and if you have never heard of or seen the movie, I can tell you it's not a very pleasant one. This American psychological horror movie was made in 1990 and is based on a story of angels, demons and their fight over human souls. The main character was a Vietnam veteran who suffered horrifying fever-like visions and got stuck in a purgatory state due to some past choices that he made. Purgatory (in Roman Catholic doctrine) is a place or state of suffering inhabited by the souls of sinners who are expiating their sins before going to heaven. In the movie, once he lets go of his past, he becomes cleansed and goes up to heaven. I couldn't believe what I was reading and had to read the summary over at least five times.

The message was direct and clear and not from the enemy but the divine. It was a warning with aspects to the reality of my circumstance and what was coming ahead if I didn't get the divine help that was absolutely necessary for my recovery. It was a warning from God, which thankfully I was still able to hear and comprehend above all the noise and the battle that was taking place at hand.

This terrifying vision prompted me to google search "churches" and "healings" in nearby areas. Only a few churches popped up in the search engine, but nothing close by. Either way it didn't matter because at this point, I was willing to drive to the ends of the earth because I knew that my life was in imminent danger. I reached out to three different congregations but was only able to do it through their website portal and or direct e-mail. Feeling hopeless and forever damned once again, I laid back down and was prepared to surrender to the consequences I selfishly created.

It was now three thirty in the afternoon and as I started to dose off in weakness again, my cell phone rang. It was an out of state area code number yet without giving a second thought I answered and said "Hello?"

A male voice on the other end answered back by saying, "Hello, this is Father James. I received an e-mail from this number requesting an immediate call back?" His voice and demeanor were firm and serious enough to know that he meant business.

I quickly introduced myself and immediately started explaining my story to him and the urgency of my situation. I could barely get my words out and felt like I couldn't speak fast enough. I decisively paused and held my breath in hopes that he would respond and not hang up.

He replied with a serious tone by asking, "You know you're playing with fire, right?"

I responded in a shameful manner saying, "Yes father, but I believed that I was helping and healing people with my gift".

"Where are you now?" He quickly replied.

I informed him that I was at my home and have been feeling spiritually ill for days and that I have not been able to work due to my spiritual sickness. I paused and held my breath, for I was certain that he would reject my plea. I mean, let's face it, spiritual forces are nothing to be reckoned with and I knew that only a special and certain type of person would be able to take that kind of task on. He then asked the magic question, "Can you come down this afternoon at five o'clock?"

It was now four thirty in the afternoon and I was no longer able to pull myself together and barely gathered enough stamina to walk outside in order to get to my car. My husband assured me and promised not to tell my son about the condition at hand and before I walked out the door, he swore to me that my son would be well taken care of while I was gone.

As I put the keys in the ignition, once again, that ominous male voice spoke to me again, and this time, it said, ***"Go fuck yourself"*** and with that I was flashed a hand giving me the finger.

My hands were now trembling, and I felt immensely faint as if I was about to go into an anaphylactic shock and or pass out. With much effort, I was able to put the keys in the ignition, and as I took off speedily to the main road, I almost hit a car in front of me that was at a complete stop at the stop sign at the end of my road.

Thankfully I never did hit that Subaru, but even if I did, it probably would have become a hit and run case because nothing was going to stop me from getting to the church to meet Father James for our five o'clock scheduled meeting. I anxiously turned the radio on in the car and blasted my favorite radio station in order to try to block out the relentlessly cruel psychic attacks again that were still lingering.

It was exactly five o'clock in the afternoon when I pulled into the church's parking lot. The car spaces were all vacant because their weekly service time varied and on this particular day it was not scheduled to start until 6:00 p.m. While parked, I cried out loud to the Lord in desperation and begged for him to save my life and in return I promised to never turn my back on him again and to never do another reading even if my life depended on it. In deep despair and remorse, I kept praying, that is until a young man dressed in a black robe with a white collar grabbed my attention.

The second Father James came into my field of vision, tears started rolling down my face uncontrollably because he surely had the presence of a saint and I knew in my heart that help was on the way. As I waited for him to signal the okay for me to come in, that evil voice attacked me once again, and this time it made sure that I was reminded of who and what I was dealing with. The demon spirit said the following: *"Do you think that seeing a priest is going to save you? You think this scares me? You're a useless piece of shit, I gave you power in exchange for your soul; you made a pact with my master, I own you and I will devour you"*

I whispered under my breath, *"Dear God, is this it? Is this how I'm going to die?* I thought for certain I was going to soil myself and vomit at the same time as my body trembled in severe distress. I now had to physically force myself to get out of the car because it felt like as if something was trying to pin me back down. With much effort I made my way over to the church's back door, still my body felt heavy and stiff, as if I was carrying heavy sand bags on the top of my shoulders. As I made my way in, the sweet aroma smell of pine trees filled my nostrils. I later learned that Father James was burning myrrh incense, which is commonly used during the Orthodox services. There was an extreme sense of comfort about it and I was more than ready to embrace God's loving presence, no matter what form it took.

The inside of the church was astoundingly breathtaking and resembled something out of a fairy tale. The paintings with the colors of yellows, golds, rich greens and purples encompassed the entire inside of the church.

The architect of the cathedral had an old eastern Greek style theme to it, and the chandelier was beyond describable, for it glittered its light as if God was shining his approval of what was about to take place.

As I stood in the doorway reluctant to move forward, Father James said with an echoed tone, "Hello, is that you Miss Beatrix?"

"Yes, I am Father, it is me." I answered.

"Come on over so we can get started," he replied, in a reassuringly confident tenor.

As I started to walk slowly towards him, my body began to tremble even more as if there were electrical currents charging my body and soul. Once I reached the center alter where Father James stood, in a solemn tone of voice he immediately started praying verses of holy scriptures over me.

My body increasingly started shaking, and although I tried to stand still as best as possible, something caused me to fall down on my knees in complete surrender. As I knelt into the floor with my eyes closed and face buried begging for mercy, I grabbed onto the tiny fibers of the churches red carpet with my dear life. As Father continued his healing prayer over me, all of the sudden this demonic appearing creature presented itself to me, and even though my eyes were closed, I could see him precisely clear. The premonition had a grayish colored skin tone, stood about eight feet tall with a cut-out -of-a-box shape look to him. It's difficult to describe, but it was like I was seeing three dimensional temporarily. It had ears which stood straight up; similar to that of a Doberman's cropped ears. Its legs were exceedingly long and its feet had claws. As this thing started dancing back and forth trying to mock me, it continuously kept vibrating back and forth into my field of vision. Once Father started sprinkling holy water over my body, I think the demon must have gotten angry because it started whipping its tail back and forth and slivering its tongue towards me. The tongue was quite long and I noticed that it split in the middle, like that of a snake. Between the attack I managed to mumble under my breath, "*Lord please forgive me for I did not know better.*"

I was ready to accept my punishment when suddenly Father stopped praying and asked me to get up. Once I stood up, I felt my jaws lock and was now unable to speak. My head became severely congested and within moments a sudden onset of flu like symptoms emerged.

I remember thinking to myself, "*Am I dead or am I alive?*" Staying motionless I tried hard to keep myself together for I did not want Father to know of what just occurred. Although I am pretty sure he knew exactly of what was going on. Once again, he resumed praying while gently placing an oil-based liquid right in the middle of my forehead. The oil had a wonderful perfume like scent and at that point he could have drenched my entire body with it and I wouldn't have cared. He further sprinkled me with holy water, said his final closing prayer, and just like that, it was over. I can't recall how many times I thanked him, but I couldn't have said it enough, for he just basically performed an exorcism.

Before leaving, I asked Father James if he has done anything like this before and without delay, he quickly said "Yes" and admitted to doing two others earlier that week.

I asked myself, "*How is it that the devil was behind all of this all along?*" And how blind was I not to see the signs earlier. I admit that I was not only dumbfounded but mortified by it all, mostly because I should have known better. I mean stuff like this has been known to happen for centuries and yet people still keep provoking the spirit world by continuously practicing psychic and or mediumship work, tarot card readings, ghost hauntings, energy healings, psychic investigations, etc. This has been known to not only invite the wicked spirits, but it also gives the opportunity to channel evil entities by the multitude into your existing life.

It was now 5:45 p.m. and with much embarrassment, I left the church with a small sense of hope. I somehow knew that this was just the beginning of my new life, and not only that, but a second chance to make things right with the Lord. I got back in my car and speeded my way back home for I wanted nothing more but to be with my family. That night a sense of calmness came over me, but I wasn't out of the woods just yet.

CHAPTER 9:
SPIRITUAL WARFARE

When an evil spirit has been driven out of a man, it roams through desert regions trying to find rest, but when it cannot find any, it says to itself, I will return to my house from which I came from, the body of the person dominated.
(Luke 11:24)

The following day, Thursday, I woke up early and although I felt slightly better, this intense gut feeling that I should return to the church was too strong to ignore. I looked on their website and saw that they had an early morning service scheduled for 7:00 a.m. Immediately I jumped out of bed and got dressed as quickly as I could and proceeded to grab my morning coffee at Dunkin Donuts, which I desperately needed not only for caffeine but for comfort, as this was my usual morning routine. I wanted nothing more but to feel as normal as possible. The shock of my new reality was now setting in and understandably so, and sadly I knew I was never going to be the same again. I arrived around 6:50 a.m. and needing to wait the 10 minutes seemed like eternity due to my excitement. I couldn't walk fast enough to get to the main entrance of the church, and no sooner then I arrived the church's bell started chiming, which meant service was starting.

Once inside I sat down quietly in the back-row benches and gratefully took in the setting of the church and the people in it. Being the shy person that I was, I wanted to talk to Father again to tell him how my night went, but at first, I hesitated. I wanted to inform him of my interest in attending the church's services and expressed to him that I didn't know how to go about it. I was having a hard time understanding the church's schedule that was posted on their website. At this point I didn't even know what religion the church was based on and whether it was Catholic or Christian. All I knew is that something was strongly drawing me back to this church and I decided that I was going to follow that inner calling. He did end up giving me the rundown of the scheduled services and although it still seemed confusing, I was going to do everything in my power to understand it and commit myself to the Lord, no matter what the cost.

By Friday I had to head back to work because I didn't have any personal and or sick time left, plus I wanted to keep myself busy from my many unwanted thoughts. I kept quiet about my experience at first but my mind seemed to do the opposite as my psychic capability was still very much open and active. The struggle to stop using my psychic capabilities wasn't going to be that simple as I now had to not only reverse, but rewire my brain's way of thinking. Through my many years of doing psychic work, I grew very comfortable with tuning in to the psychic realm with a snap of a finger and now I had to make the impossible happen and disengage my entire compilation of psychic work. How the heck was I going to make myself become un-psychic and rid my psychic burdens? Nevertheless, try to erase the memories and make it non-existent as if it never happened.

Feeling much disgrace and regret I knew that the only way out was to totally surrender to the Lord and let him lead the way. Besides, it has been a long time coming for me to get to know the real God intimately, and that time was now. In my heart of hearts, I knew that in order for this to really work I had to stand firm in the presence of God and not grow impatient with his timing. I was desperate and felt absolutely hopeless because I had no idea of what was going to become of me, but I did know one thing for sure, I absolutely wanted nothing to do with mysticism or new age spirituality.

Still, I found myself constantly trying to dodge and block the influx of psychic information that was redundantly being presented to me. I was growing very tired of the persistent psychological mayhem and the unwanted spirit communication, meanwhile, I had to try my best to remain calm and act normal as if nothing was happening inside and or around me. Inevitably, I eventually had to come clean and confess to people and friends that I was no longer interested in doing psychic work because people were still coming out of the woodworks trying to request appointments for readings, and it seemed that the number of requests were now increasingly larger in numbers than ever before. It disgusted me to know that all this time I had not only been deceived but maliciously tricked into, what I would call, a soul contract with the devil. I had to face the music and accept the cold hard truth about the enemy and his tactics of duplicity and how he uses gifted people, such as myself, to lure us into his works of mysticism and new age by catfishing the weak and the lost. Satan and his legion of demons basically hijacked my intuitive gift and took advantage of my psychic vulnerability. Furthermore, I also ended up losing lots of friendships throughout the transition and I quickly came to the realization that some of these friendships were solely based on my gift and that this was God's way of cleaning house and the tarnished people within it.

As I continued to be tormented with frightening visions, it became evident that the enemy was still trying to pursue me. He was unambiguously trying to subdue my soul with inflictions of fear and continuously casted feelings of unworthiness upon my existence. I also learned soon after that once you turn your back on Satan and his legions, they will surely retaliate and aggressively turn on you. I also came to the understanding that once you become aware of the sham and the malicious trickery, your so-called spirit friends will not only become your enemies but your worst nightmare. The relentless spiritual bullying was starting to take a toll on my health, however God was going to make sure that I was going to come out of this alive and fully reformed from the sins of life, although for me, it didn't seem possible at the time.

I was constantly praying like a mad woman and figuratively became a prayer warrior. The more unraveled I became the more I would find myself in psychological pain. I realize that part of that struggle came from the new awareness that I now suffered with consciously as well as spiritually. I eventually had to start taking prescription strength sleeping pills just so I could get some peace and rest from it all, thus at this point I was still in the early stages of my recovery phase. My emotions were getting the best of me and rightfully so, hence I had just experienced a close encounter with evil himself. My monkey mind was driving me crazy and my bouts of depression, anger and hopelessness seemed to continuously drag me down. I felt uncomfortable being in my own skin and hated waking up to the reality of my life and its new existence.

I couldn't wrap my head around the extent of such evil even though it has been written for centuries. Ironically until it happens to one of us, we just ignore the seriousness and the consequences that follow. The following week, after the exorcism, being the way things were progressing, I continued to feel defeated as if God had banned me from his scope of love, although that wasn't the case at all. I felt utterly broken as if I had been chewed up, spit out and left for dead. My life was falling apart and my paradigm system of beliefs was now burned to the ground. I felt like I had been reborn all over again, and life seemed more like a stranger rather than a friend. However, that was all about to change, for God was about set things straight and reveal his plan for me.

It was another long day at the office and after getting home and eating dinner I made the decision to go to bed early because I felt exhausted and sleepy by early evening. I took my sleeping pill earlier than usual and said goodnight to my husband and my son, and crashed into bed.

I woke up around 1:00 a.m. to use the bathroom and went right back to bed. As I slowly started dosing off to sleep, I became aware of the loud buzzing noise in my ear, which usually means that a message was about to come. I didn't have the energy to fight it because the sleeping pill was still in effect, so I had no choice but to listen. I was given the following information which I was not prepared to hear or accept on this particular night.

1. **You have been sanctified and delivered from evil.**

2. **You have been chosen to minister the truth and to speak sermons.**

3. **You have been ordained to preach this truth in order to help Father, our creator, save more souls.**

I could not comprehend of what I was hearing, never mind understand the language. I have never heard these terms before; *What did sanctify and ordained even mean? And out of all people, why have I been chosen?* I felt unworthy of all this; I definitely wasn't about to become a female priest, yet I knew in my heart that I needed to answer God's call, I mean it's the least I could do after all that he has done for me. Being skeptical and feeling dumbfounded, I had absolutely no idea of what to make of all this and so I foolishly attempted to plead with the Lord with prayer and begged God to choose someone else. The first thing I did upon waking was google the words sanctified, sermons and ordained on my iPhone. I was amazed and confused by what these words represented and knew in my heart that this message was from a divine source and not an evil one. I can surely attest that the enemy would not want me to preach God's truth and recruiting me to help save souls on behalf of the Lord is certainly not something that the devil would have on his agenda. Still struggling to feel normal and sane I forced myself to ignore the message, and honestly, this was not something that I was prepared to hear at the time. I hoped that if I rejected the message it would all just go away, and so that is exactly what I did, I defied it.

However, as we know it, God always has the last word, and this time he was going to make sure that I heard his message loud and clear. Within the next few weeks, I experienced another episode similar to the previous one and received the following message;

1. **You have been exalted and redeemed.**

2. **Minister in the name of the Lord, anointed one.**

3. **Don't be afraid; they left quickly, the demons have fled.**

4. **This is your destiny; a true calling.**

5. **The rope has been dislodged as you are now venerated.**

That morning when I awoke, I felt an immense sense of relief as if a huge burden has been lifted off my shoulders. I now believed God's message and didn't feel threatened or feared by the experience. It was like a light bulb had gone off and I knew in my heart that I was going to be okay. The battle ahead was clear but knowing that God would be with me and all around me this time around, in conclusion, prevented me from withstanding his call. I suddenly understood just exactly what the Lord was trying to convey and deep down inside, I think it's what I was trying to do all along, except I went about it in all the wrong ways.

I now felt an intense need to surrender to God's will but not before dealing with what was to come as a secondary consequence to my actions. I started having random episodes of PTSD, also known as "post-traumatic syndrome disorder. The attacks of anxiety and panic was something I was going to have to adjust to temporarily, as it was now happening on a daily basis. From the time I'd awake to the time I went to bed, I would endure at least 6-8 episodes of sudden onsets of fear and panic, and at times without reason. *But was it really without reason?* Absolutely not, I knew all too well of whom the culprit was behind my suffering and how the dark angels were using their heinous forces of inflictions by not only attacking the mind but also the heart and soul, in a manipulative and conjuring way. The devil was still working hard to wear me down and eventually It started to feel like I was paddling backwards rather than forward with my recovery.

I had to muster up the courage to seek professional help, but I was also going to have to keep the detail of my experiences to a bare minimum because there was a strong possibility that I was going to be misunderstood and or misdiagnosed at best due to the nature of my case. I was quite surprised to learn that my therapist was strong in faith, and not only that, he knew exactly of the kind of ordeal I was experiencing. He had no intention of labeling me psychotic or schizophrenic because he himself also had a similar experience with the evil one. He was very familiar with spiritual warfare and expressed his concern about the situation in a compassionate manner. He even helped answer and clarify the many questions and doubts I still had about the bible. The chances of me finding a therapist like this was slim to none, but only because of God did that slim chance become a fat chance. My loving Father and Creator was not going to let me slip through his fingers this time around, at least not under his watch. With persistent prayer, a lot of bible reading and God's guidance, I was finally on the fast track to healing and salvation.

Below are some examples of what a psychic attack feels like and what the devil tried to use on me during my spiritual warfare; I am including this piece of information in hopes that I can help others to recognize what a spiritual warfare might look like: Keep in mind that circumstances could vary.

1. **Hearing and thinking foul language and or degrading comments that are intentionally inflicted against you.**

2. **Flashing visions of demonic faces; images of characters from horror movies, especially the ones that have frightened you the most in the past.**

3. **Sleep deprivation followed by ghoulish bad dreams and or night terrors.**

4. **Constant bad thoughts without reasoning, such as suicide, infliction of self-harm and hopelessness followed by feelings of despair and doom.**

5. **Sudden offensive odors that smell rotten or decomposing.**

6. **Intrusive psychic powers and or visions.**

7. **Paralytic out of body experiences followed by extreme bouts of fear, specifically related to the knowing and or feeling of an evil entities' presence.**

8. **Invisible spiritual forces provoking you sexually during deep stages of sleep.**

9. **Unexplained supernatural occurrences.**

10. **Increased feelings of temptations to sin without reason.**

CHAPTER 10:
SALVATION

*"Amazing grace, how sweet the sound
that saved a wretch like me.
I once was lost, but now am found
I was blind but now I see."*

Before I move on to my final stages of salvation, I must mention an important piece of information that will make more sense later in the story. In the midst of my spiritual warfare I started seeing visions of light brown colored mushrooms, specifically the ones that grow on the barks of trees, a type of mushroom that has a medium size top to them with wrinkled round edges. I had absolutely no idea what its significance meant and at the time I didn't bother questioning it, never mind make any sense of it. It was the least of my worries for I obviously had bigger fish to fry. I had to trust that it would be revealed to me eventually, which it was, but on God's time, not mine.

It was now October and fall was in full bloom with it's beautiful autumn harvest. It was my fifth time attending the Sunday service at the "All Saints" Orthodox church and I had no intention of straying. I wasn't new to the idea of religious conversion, but I didn't know much about the Orthodox religion and have never known of its existence until now. I was more than willing to learn about their tradition and eager to understand the worship. From the first moment I stepped foot in the church I was in love and it wouldn't be long before becoming mesmerized by their byzantine themed liturgy services. In addition, I was very grateful for Father James and his role in my salvation. Right from the start there seemed to be something very majestic about the parish and I felt honored to be part of it. On one particular Sunday, while reading through the service pamphlet, I noticed that there were two pierogi workshops scheduled to take place in the last two weeks of October.

The church needed help in preparing food for their big yearly event called the "Russian Bazaar Tea Room" and I was more than happy to help. It was early evening on a Friday night and the first workshop was scheduled to start at 6:00 p.m. I was nervous because I didn't know anybody personally, plus I have always been shy in new social settings. The people there that night were friendly but they also seemed surprised by my presence. I just stayed focused and did my best to help with whatever was needed, including making dough and boiling potatoes.

I had to work the next morning but that didn't stop me from staying late into the night. I was quite humbled by the thought that I was able to partake in carrying out God's work that night and before I left, I agreed to help out in the next scheduled workshop. It was the Friday before Halloween and I arrived early with eagerness and wasted no time with the list of things that needed to be done. By the end of the night we had successfully stuffed, pinched, and packaged over 200 pierogis. The workshop was coming to a close and it was now time to clean up.

I sprayed down the stainless steel counter top and realized that I needed some dry paper towel in order to finish the job. I turned around and went to reach for the towel but there was a clear food bag in the way, and as I got closer to see what the bag contained, suddenly this overwhelming feeling of joy overcame my well-being and immediately my eyes started watering. What I saw in the food bag would not only draw me closer to God but also create a new sense of trust, faith and hope, with aspects to what he had planned out for me. The bag contained dried mushrooms, and they weren't just any kind of mushrooms but the same exact ones that I have been envisioning since my exorcism. These mushrooms were the same porcini super mushrooms that God was cluing me in with, which I believe, was a confirmation and a sign of approval with aspects to the Orthodox faith and its religion.

I suddenly realized that this is exactly where the Lord intended for me to be and came to the conclusion that the Lord used this specific serendipity of a moment to keep me aligned with his will and purpose. The message was undeniable clear and although I appeared to be calm on the outside, on the inside I was screaming with joy. I can't describe the immense feeling of relief that I felt at that exact moment but what I can tell you is that it felt like a huge weight was lifted off my shoulder. I now knew the reasons as to why I kept seeing these mushrooms and it gave me a peace of mind to know that I was finally on God's direct path.

As I began to look further into Orthodoxy and its practices I uncovered and stumbled upon a crucial detail within its history which would essentially ignite the passion of Christ in me. I discovered that Saint Peter, whom was also called "The Rock" was the originate co-founder of Orthodoxy and learned that he established this Christian movement directly after Jesus's death. This was a huge revelation for me because as you have come to know earlier in my story, Saint Peter is the one that manifested himself to me through an image on an index card. Once I put two and two together it suddenly dawned on me as to why this famous saint was hovering over me and the pieces of the puzzle that were once a big mess of confusion were now finally coming together and becoming very significant.

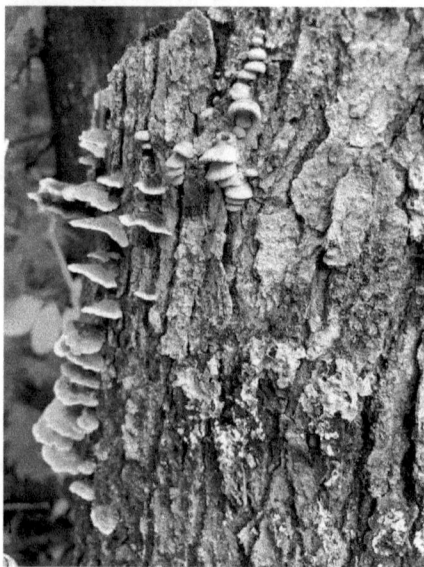

The Lord your God is with you, the mighty warrior who saves. He will take great delight in you; in his love he will no longer rebuke you, but will rejoice over you with singing.
(Zephaniah 3:17)

I thought I had some hands-on experience with reading the bible but obviously not, since I had no clue of whom Saint Peter was, that is until now. I know it sounds ridiculous but I'm being totally honest here. *How could I not know about Saint Peter?* I mean, he played a remarkably huge roll in the life of Jesus; as a matter of fact, many churches are now named after him as an honor of remembrance. I believe that Saint Peter was one of the many divine protectors who kept me safe throughout my dangerous ordeal. In the beginning this was hard for me to process spiritually because I felt unworthy of his presence and surely I wasn't the only person on this planet that he has guided. But on the other hand, it became undeniably clear that I had been chosen, one out of many, to carry out God's will and truth. It was extremely reassuring to know that I was not only good enough in God's eyes but also considered a valuable tool for his purpose, for he obviously saw something in me that I never did.

Once I understood this, I believe, is when the Lord touched me with his holy spirit. It's really hard to explain the experience, a person must directly experience it for himself in order to understand the effects of this kind of enlightenment. I now couldn't bear the thought of Jesus without getting teary eyed and feeling euphorically happy. I have never before experienced anything like it and probably won't ever again, besides, I won't need to because the gift of the holy spirit is a permanent exchange between God and man. Our Father and creator finally got my full and undivided attention and deservingly so. I accepted my fate and was now able and ready to surrender myself to God's will and his call. One trouble still remained though - my relentless enemy. I had to learn and try to figure out how to effectively block and filter out the devil's whispered lies over God's divine calling. This was not going to be easy because as we know it, the devil is the master of illusions.

I did start noticing distinctions between the two, specifically with colors. When receiving messages from truth, it's always warm and bright in pigment and hue, while the enemy's is always gray and dark. The divine's light is always bright and projected in full screen while the devil's is intrusive, random and vibrational without color. Either way, no matter where the message came from, it was obvious that I still had the gift. However, I knew that I had to keep this gift hidden and away from the world because it is probably meant to be used as a compass for our own personal journey in life rather than to prophecies.

63

By November of 2017 I was finally starting to feel relief from the heaviness of my painful experience. I was steadily becoming stronger and more confident with my new Christ like mind. Still being committed to daily prayer and my new-founded faith, I was still continuously attending church every Sunday. While progressing on my journey to redemption, once again, I started experiencing a recurrent vision from God. *How did I know that it was from the divine?* Because it was bright, beautiful and full of warm colors. The choreography was always consistent with the colors of Christmas. These new visions appeared only at night while dosing off to sleep.

The images presented came in a multitude of forms, including, butterflies, fireworks and even a hot air balloon. There was something soothing and comforting about these visions and I knew that it meant something of real importance. I would still find myself frightened by it at times but I also knew that this was coming directly from God and that he was speaking to me in ways that I could only comprehend. It would take another book for me to write a compilation of my divine experiences, therefore, I am only going to mention the few that essentially tie this story together.

Throughout my conversion I experienced continuous support spiritually not only from God but from the church members as well. I found it to be simple but challenging at times because like any other religion, one must learn to understand the history and their intimate religious views before given the opportunity to get baptized. Knowing that this was a long time coming I quickly made the choice to become a catechumen, also known as Christian convert, who is under instruction before baptism. If a person has been previously baptized by another congregation outside of Orthodoxy, then a chrismation would be in order.

Chrismation (sometimes called confirmation) is considered to be a sacrament or mystery in the Eastern Orthodox and or Eastern Catholic religion. If a person wants to receive a chrismation, he or she will have to undergo an anointment process, which can only be performed by a priest in a church. This holy mystery and granting of the holy spirit are given to us through the rite of initiation and by being anointed with chrism oil. The oil consists of a mixture of sweet-smelling substance and pure olive oil. I obviously fell under the full submerged under water baptism category since I was never baptized as a child or an adult.

Happily, I moved forward with the decision to get baptized and to become a proud Orthodox Christian. I felt honored to have been given the opportunity to do so. It was an intensely emotional period for me but that didn't stop me from attending the five required study classes, which I successfully finished in just a few short four weeks. There were three of us at the time (catechumens) and surprisingly Father James conducted the class himself. Before being scheduled for my baptism, I also had to go through a painful admission process called confession. Whenever the topic came up for discussion, my throat would choke and my eyes welled up with tears.

I don't know what I was afraid of, after all, God was willing and ready to forgive me and my past, yet I wasn't quite ready to forgive myself. After the confession I remember how free I felt not only in my heart but also in mind and soul, as if the weight of the world has been lifted. I felt proud of my accomplishment and couldn't wait for Father to schedule my baptism.

It was the week before Christmas on a Saturday morning and as I headed out to run some errands, I got a notification of an urgent e-mail from Father James titled "baptism". My heart raced as I opened the e-mail message because I knew that the information was going to include the date of my scheduled baptism. I have been looking forward to hearing this news for quite some time, and now here it was.

I bypassed most of the contents in the message because I was more worried about the names and dates of the next upcoming scheduled baptisms. Lo and behold, my baptism was scheduled to take place on December 25th at 8:30 am which we all know is Christmas day! I couldn't believe it, not only was it going to take place on the most important day of the year, but I now understood as to why I kept seeing the Christmas themed colored images. I was absolutely beside myself about this revelation and couldn't wait to tell my husband about the news and the correlation between my visions and God's timing. It was now more than obvious of how quickly the Lord acted once I had rebuked the evil one, and without further delay, he wanted to make sure that I stay the course to salvation. I can't recall a time where I experienced such love mostly because I have never truly surrendered myself to our Creator, until now.

What I ultimately learned from this experience is not only God's true love and existence but also the unconditional love, patience and dedication that he holds for all mankind. I don't think that God ever gave up on the hopes of my salvation, rather, he just had to let me feel the burn for a little while as a consequence to the seriousness of my actions. This new level of awakening not only reinstalled my respect and fear towards God but it also relinquished my lost relationship with him and his glory. Had I not experienced this painful revelation I would of never have come to know of just how fine the boundaries are between good and evil.

Photograph of me praying in a park under a shrine 2018.

After the baptism my heart was anew and It felt like I had been given a new pair of eyes. Having been newly transformed I became more seemingly perplexed by the evilness of the world and my sensitivity towards the weak and the suffering turned up a few notches.

I was supposed to feel happy and free, thus I have been delivered and saved from the evil one, yet I felt sad and dampened by the reality of this life on earth. I eventually grew to understand the reasons behind my emotional state and realized that when somebody hands over their life and purpose to Jesus, they will also become minded like Jesus. The countless number of lost souls walking around was more evident to me than ever before and this sudden urge to preach the good news became an undeniably loud calling in my heart.

Knowing that I could never become a priest or a preacher, I didn't know what to do with my feelings about all this. In addition, I didn't want to fall prey to the devil's schemes again and so I prayed on it and patiently waited for an answer.

I didn't try to force an answer like I would have in the past, I now solely relied on God's guidance and timing. I knew that if God had something to say, he would make it known and say it in his own space and time. It was a cold evening and I went to bed early due to feeling under the weather. I finished my nightly prayer and fell asleep swiftly due to exhaustion. Still suffering from bouts of insomnia, it wasn't unusual for me to not sleep throughout the night. I awoke around 2:30 a.m. one morning and decided to scroll Facebook so I could tire myself back to sleep.

Within a short ten-minute time period I became drowsy again and as I tried dosing off to sleep, I heard the word *"catalyst."*

At first, I ignored it, which of course wasn't going to work, because no sooner then I started dosing off again, the voice said it again, *"Christian catalyst."*

What in the world does this mean? Doesn't catalyst refer to chemistry and or chemical reactions? Like the ones we learn about in science class?

I immediately googled Christian catalyst. The definition and its meaning are as follows:

- *There must be the presence of a catalyst who is full of Christ.*

- *One who drinks deeply from the word of God.*

- *Seeks to please God rather than men.*

- *Gets deeply involved in the lives of others.*

- *Sets the proper example and inspire people to live for the Lord.*

Wow! Once again, I knew that God was up to something because I have never heard of these terms before and God always seems to use sophisticated language with me when he spoke. *What was I supposed to do with this message? Was this what God wanted me to do or was he telling me whom I was becoming?* That weekend my inspiration drove me to go to a local Christian book store in town and I ended up purchasing a bunch of wooden cross necklaces and a couple of small prayer books. I placed them in my purse just in case I came across the opportunity to preach the truth in relevance to my experience. I desperately wanted to help God save more souls and continuously prayed for him to send people my way so he could use me as a tool, but strictly for his will. Within a two-month period I ended up handing out at least 20 wooden cross necklaces, 3 prayer books and one bible. Feeling more at ease with my experience I started becoming more vocal about my salvation and eventually mustered up the courage to share my story with a couple of people.

I was deeply touched by their compassion during my testimony and was amazed of how receptive they were to the tangible evidence I had presented. It felt righteously good to preach the truth and to expose the work of the evil one in my own unique non-traditional way. Meanwhile the presence of Christ and Saint Peter continued to intensify in the everyday reality of my life and it wouldn't be until May of 2018 that God would make a powerful revelation in my life to show that he was not only listening to my prayers but also answering them. As I started to grow accustomed to my routine of constant prayer, I was also subconsciously hoping that it was making a difference.

It was now May of 2018, and I started having issues with my esophagus and couldn't get rid of my chronic heartburn. The over the counter products no longer seemed to help and so I made an appointment with a gastroenterologist specialist. The appointment was scheduled to take place Thursday, May 10, and I made sure to arrive early because I was anxious about my persistent esophageal reflex.

As I sat waiting to be called in, I decided to make my time useful and so I started reading prayer hymns from my little blue Orthodox prayer book, which I carried with me all the time. I only had to wait 15 minutes before my name was called and I remember feeling impressed with the short wait time.

Once I made it into the exam room it wouldn't be long before the provider, a beautiful young lady, entered the room and introduced herself as Connie. She was a physician assistant under the guidance of a medical director and seemed not only competent in her role but compassionate with regards to my concerns. She interviewed me with a bunch of medical questions and made a couple of recommendations pertaining to diet and medication. The appointment seemed normal and routine at first but that was about to quickly change as the unthinkable happened.

In the midst of our encounter Connie and I unexpectedly got on the subject of Jesus and God. I even ended up talking about my experience and couldn't help myself from going into full preach mode. She must have been touched by my story because she then confided in me of how she has been trying for a baby for years but to no avail. She further told me that she had gone through numerous infertility treatments and tried every tactic in the book in hopes of conception.

I quickly slid off the table and offered her a prayer, specifically a virgin Mary prayer intended for mothers who were trying to conceive. I left the office feeling nervous because I had never done anything strange like this before plus, I didn't want to let her down since I knew that ultimately the results were all in God's hands.

I left the office in prayer and begged God to help this young woman out. I got in my car and turned the radio on and a song from the band called "*Ace of Base*" was playing on the radio. The song is called *All that she wants* and is based on a woman wanting a baby. Being familiar with God's humor, the chances of me hearing this old song on a popular pop radio station right after a prayer session for conception was slim to none. The song originally came out in 1992. I couldn't help but to giggle with joy in this serendipitous moment because it was obvious that God was about to answer my prayer.

I continued to pray for Connie and it wouldn't be until the end of May that I would learn of her pregnancy. As a matter of fact, she ended up driving to my place of work on a Friday because she wanted to tell me this great news in person. We were ecstatic and beyond belief with the experience of this newly acquired miracle, and our excitement level seemed to be the same but obviously for different reasons. Before she left the office, we prayed again but this time for a safe and healthy delivery and she also promised to bring the baby in once he or she was born.

What I learned about that experience is that I could still help people, like the way I use to when I was a psychic/medium, but this time righteously and only with God and the power of prayer. Even though it's been just over a year since my baptism, sometimes I still find myself in fear of my experience. When in doubt I always pray for reassurance and never has God denied my requests. I can genuinely say that I still wholeheartedly appreciate Gods love and mercy and couldn't imagine my life without Him.

CHAPTER 11:
REVELATION

"Put on the full armor of God, so that you can take your stand against the devil's schemes. for our struggle is not against flesh and blood, but against the rulers, against authorities, against the powers of this dark world and against the spiritual forces of evil. Therefore, put on the full armor of God, so that when the day of evil comes, you may be able to stand your ground, and after you have done everything, to stand. in addition to all this, take up the shield of faith, with which you can extinguish all the flaming arrows of the evil one. Take the helmet of salvation and the sword of the spirit, which is the word of God"
(Ephesians 6:11-17)

I must say it again: I had no intention of writing this book, certainly not publishing it. I have never written a book previous to this one and don't plan on doing so in the future. I wrote this book for no other reason than to answer God's loving command and to fulfill his will. My Lord and Savior is persistent, he never gave up on my ignorance and fear with aspects to writing this testimony. He sent visions and dreams often enough to the point where I could no longer ignore his request. I mention this because I feel it is important for the reader to know of just how this book came about. In my heart, I want nothing more but to please the Lord and the only thing I care about besides my family is what he thinks of me.

As you can see, I answered his call even though I dreaded the idea of having to relive the experience once again. I truly believe that God is going to use my truth as a tool to help others who are deemed in very similar situations, even those who have already gone too far.

God has been known to use the weary and the broken, such as myself, specifically for his will and purpose for centuries. Take for example the biblical story of "*Saul of Tarsus*", who was a brutal persecutor of Christians, who also killed hundreds of innocent Jews and Jesus believers before his ultimate divine encounter with Jesus Christ. He eventually became to be known as "**Paul the Apostle**" and his surviving letters ended up having an enormous influence on subsequent Christianity and secured his place as one of the greatest religious leaders of all time. As a matter of fact, of the 27 books in the New Testament, 13 have been attributed to Paul and his apostleship.

It takes a pretty powerful life altering experience for someone to change from being a killer of Christians to then suddenly becoming a disciple of Christ. It's the same exact thing that I strongly believe happened to me but with different circumstances. The experience was immensely divine and sudden which ultimately lead me to my new conviction and reasoning. My passion continuously flickers for the Lord and I still pray daily as a reminder of just how powerful and merciful God still is. Paul's conviction eventually led him to be martyred (killed for his faith) in his sixties. (*Wikipedia/wiki/Paul the Apostle*).

Paul the Apostle in Prison, writing his letter, one of many, to the Ephesians.

During the next 20 years or so after his divine encounter, he even established several churches in Asia Minor and at least three in Europe, including the church at Corinth. This man obviously had such a revolutionary experience with Christ that it ultimately brought him from hating and killing Christians to ministering and becoming an elite ambassador for Christ.

In another powerful redemption of faith and sudden conversion was an Islamic militant in the middle east who was known for his brutal killing of Christians. After dreaming of a man in white and receiving a very vivid message, where Jesus said to him, "You are killing my people" the militant started feeling sick and very uneasy about his doings. The last victim that he killed before his conversion threw a bible at him before being beheaded. The ISIS fighter picked the bible up, took it with him and actually started reading it. In another dream, Jesus asked the man to follow him and directed the ISIS militant to become a follower of Christ and to be discipled. After these dramatic altering encounters, the violent fighter confessed his conversion to Christianity. (christiantoday.com/ISIS militant converts to Christianity after meeting Jesus in a dream).

How about the fascinating true story of an atheist journalist, who after going on a mission to discredit the existence of Jesus, ultimately gets led to the Lord and even becomes a preaching minister. (*The Case for Christ* 2017 movie).

Joan of Arc is another historical true story of a young girl who had a series of divine visions which ultimately ignited her passion and conviction in the power of God. Joan of Arc who was nicknamed "The Maid of Orléans," is considered a heroine of France for her role during the Lancastrian phase of the Hundred Years' War, and was later canonized as a Roman Catholic saint. She was only nineteen years old when she was sentenced to death and burned on a stake as a martyr.[1]

"One life is all we have and we live it as we believe in living it. But to sacrifice what you are and to live without belief, that is a fate more terrible than dying."
–Joan of Arc

Saint Mary of Egypt is another great example of conviction and of how divine encounters lead sinners to serve the Lord until their last breath. Saint Mary of Egypt is another great example of just how powerful a leading encounter with the holy spirit can be in a person's life and the permanent psychological effects it inflicts.

Mary began her life as a young woman who followed the passions of the body, running away from her parents at age twelve and settled herself in Alexandria. There she lived as a harlot for seventeen years, refusing money from the men that she copulated with, instead living by begging and spinning flax.

---

[1] https://www.biographyonline.net/women/joan-of-arc

One day, however, she met a group of young men heading toward the sea to sail to Jerusalem for the veneration of the Holy Cross. Mary went along for the ride, seducing the men as they traveled for the fun of it. But when the group reached Jerusalem and actually went towards the church, Mary was prohibited from entering by an unseen force. After three attempts, she stopped yet remained outside on the church patio, where she looked up and saw an icon of the virgin Mary. She began to weep and prayed with all her might to the virgin Mary in hopes that she might allow her to see the one true cross and in exchange she made a promise that she would renounce her worldly desires and go wherever the holy divine spirit may lead her.

After this heart-felt conversion at the doors of the church, she fled into the desert to live as an ascetic. She survived for many years on just bread alone and scarce herbs from the land. For many years, Mary was tormented by old fleshy sexual desires and passions. After years of temptation, however, she overcame the passions and stayed determined to stay true to her promise that she made many years ago to the virgin Mary.

I never use to understand such passion until I experienced it personally myself. Now, when I come across such stories it actually puts a smile on my face because I know exactly what certainty they experienced and the faith they are talking about. These are minute examples of Gods power out of the thousands that have happened in the past or are currently happening now. Maybe such testimonies aren't ready to be revealed to the public yet, and sadly some will never bring it to light.

BRINGING MY STORY TO THE TABLE

On August 16, 2018 I had just finished working out at my local gym. I proceeded to the girl's locker room so I could rinse my face and wash my hands. As I stood there in front of the mirror trying to dry off, I caught a glimpse of a shiny small pocket-sized booklet sitting to my left by the blow dryer that was attached to the wall. I got curious and after I finished drying my hands off, I stepped over to see what the book was about.

The cover of the booklet was glossed with a shiny film and the image on the front portrayed a person standing in a pair of blue jeans on a pavement road. On the cover was also a painted thick white arrow pointing forward. Oddly the booklet didn't have a title and so I opened it to see what this mysterious book was about. What I read next surged me to have an immediate conversation with God, which then lead to a sequence of events compelling me to share my story. The contents read as follows:

"You are holding a true story in your hands"

As I stood there flabbergasted, I quickly came to the conclusion that this was another God moment. I understood the message and knew that the holy spirit was once again trying to encourage and motivate me to write my testimony, but this time the Lord went above and beyond to make sure that the message was loud and clear. Without hesitation I quickly grabbed the little booklet and briskly left the gym and quickly ran to my car.

As I sat there in silence staring at the night sky trying to gather my scattered thoughts, I was suddenly over taken by a strong desire to pray and didn't want to wait until I got home. I looked around to make sure that nobody was around because I always considered prayer sacred and private, and once I saw that it was safe, I prayed the following with a true heartfelt notion:

"Father, I know that you want me to write this book and have been telling me to do so for months now. Father, I don't know how to write a book, I don't know how to go about the process or where to begin, but if you give me the help and the means, I promise not to let you down. Father, I need your divine guidance and the protection from the evil one so I can stay strong and confident. Who is going to believe me? I am scared to do this Father… I am scared. In the name of the Father, and of the Son and of the Holy Spirit…Amen"

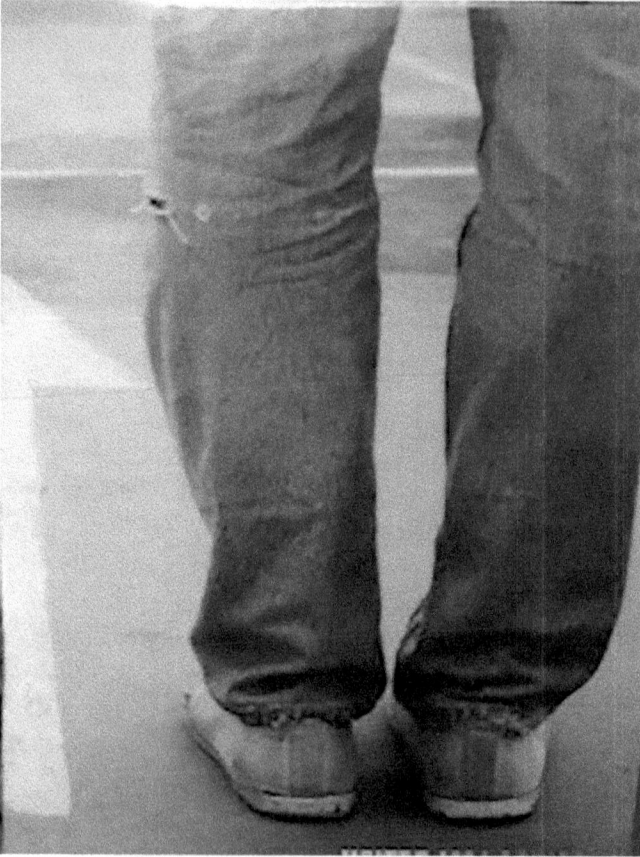

YOU ARE HOLDING A TRUE STORY IN YOUR HANDS.

Actual photos of the small booklet.

The next day at work I was going about my business as usual and because I work in a doctor's office I interact with a multitude of patients throughout the day. However, this day was going to prove to be a bit different because God's plan to answer my prayer came sooner than I had expected. It was around 10:00 am and I eagerly bought in the next scheduled patient by the name of Michael into the exam room. I finished the intake procedure and preceded to let the doctor know that her next patient was ready to be examined. This kind of routine was normal and nothing seemed out of the ordinary, that is until the three of us got to talking.

Making conversation with patients can be pretty easy in this line of work because people are usually in a position where they are more than willing to express concerns. The visit was coming to a close and once I finished scribing (taking notes) I decided to sit down because my legs were quite sore from the workout at the gym the night before. While the patient and the doctor continued talking, I slowly began to zone out by staring out the windows of the exam room. Suddenly their voices seemed to get louder and I suddenly heard the patient say, "*I am an author of a book based on a true story.*"

Regaining my focus with what was now placed in front of me I instantly interrupted the conversation by acknowledging his comment. I then engaged him with a direct eye contact in hopes of grabbing his undivided attention. I was jittering with excitement and immediately knew that God had sent this person my way for a very important reason. Barely given Michael the chance for a response, he still managed to squeeze a few words in between my run-on sentences and nervous energy.

He not only offered his guidance but also agreed to help with the steps that I needed to take to get it published. *Wow! I mean seriously? How great is God when it comes to miracles?* Greater than I could have ever imagined, as he evidently turned a simple routine office visit into a huge powerful serendipity moment. For a quick second the attention turned on me and I was asked the obvious question of whether I was looking to write my own true story. This sudden heave of confidence overcame my self-control because I knew that Michael was purposefully meant to meet me that very day and once again God's divine intervention was unraveling right before my eyes. Before Michael left, we not only exchanged phone numbers but he also gave me a copy of his book titled "A *Promise to Astrid*" which by the way, I read in two short days and is available for purchase on *Amazon.com*.

I remained ecstatic for the rest of the day by his promise of calling me and by the next morning that is exactly what he did. Here I am a few months later, and I am finishing up my first draft. I can attest that I wouldn't have been able to write down such intricate details of my experience in such a short amount of time without God's support and guidance and not only that, in a recent vision I was specifically instructed by the Lord to title my book as **Devil's Sport** and for good reasons. It might be deceiving to some because one might think that the book is about how to play the devil's sport rather than its real meaning, which is, how the devil plays us as a sport. The book cover was also guided by the divine after a quick prayer request. Both ideas were explicitly clear when God gave his recommendations and I give all the credit to him and only him. Either way I followed our God's command and trust that he will put this book in the hands of those that desperately need his salvation.

I am happy to say that since my baptism, my recurrent nightmares of evil spirits and possessions have totally ceased. Subconsciously the torment has stopped and my terrifying experiences with the evil entity no longer exist. Don't get me wrong, just because I converted to Christianity does not exempt me from future spiritual attacks but with the power of Jesus Christ and prayer, I am no longer afraid. Anytime fear (devil) tries inflicting feelings of dread with threating gestures, I immediately call on the Lord which promptly subdues the evil away. The Lord's loving interaction with me is now undeniably loud and clear and my conviction about his existence gets stronger by the day.

Even when I have questions that I don't dare to pray about, God still answers them unexpectedly. For example, I have been wanting to take college courses on theology and apologetics but realistically I knew that I couldn't afford it. I was pondering on the idea for a couple of days but couldn't muster up the courage to ask God for assistance because I felt selfish about it, besides, I felt that I should be more focused on praying for the suffering rather than ponder on my own personal request of a college tuition.

One night I was scrolling through videos on the internet on topics of evangelism but nothing seemed to grab my attention. I remember feeling sad about it and decided not to pursue it further because it seemed hopeless to attain. The next morning while driving to work on the highway a white 18-wheeler tractor trailer decided to cut in front of me, probably because I was driving too slow for his liking. I started to focus in on the back of the truck to see what company the jerk worked for but there was no company advertising, but only two words written in large black bold letters that said "FREE CLASSES". I was still startled at that given moment and didn't give a second thought to its message. However, once I arrived at work it suddenly dawned on me that this was divine guidance, although at first, I felt hesitant to act on it as such, mostly due to fear.

To make the long story short, a couple of days later I did google search free classes and I am now happily enrolled in a free bible certificate and apologetic course. To some people it might have been common sense to search for these free classes in the first place but for me that didn't even cross my mind. The moral of this incident is to show how God has the capability to guide us in unique ways and when we start living righteously and in sync with the truth and his will, the Lord's presence and existence will become irrefutably surreal.

Another great example of God's work happened in my life as follows:

I have been job searching for a few months with no avail. I decided to seek work in a field different than the one that I have been dedicated to all my life. A few weeks into searching for a veterinary position I wasn't getting any responses from any employers.

I don't blame them, usually you have to have at least one year of experience in the field or at least be a new graduate of animal sciences for them to glance or even consider your credentials. I had none of these attributes and decided to throw in the towel.

A week after ceasing and giving up on job searching something occurred that only could have taken place with divine intervention. It was a typical day at work and the day was coming to a close. I took in the last patient of the day and proceeded to clean the exam rooms that we used that day. I was interrupted and asked to help chaperone the skin exam on the patient that I took in a few minutes earlier.

Feeling annoyed and tired I headed into the exam room to assist the provider assigned to the appointment. Once in the room I did my usual routine duties and started charting the specifics of the exam. I took a notice to her last name, specifically because she had the same last name as the veterinarian doctor I have been using for my horses. I have two beautiful senior horses that I rescued and they both require yearly vaccinations and teeth cleaning.

I said to her; "Wait a minute here, is your dad a veterinarian?"

Before I could ask her another question, she said; "Yes he is, and I am his daughter and office manager."

Without thinking, I blurted out and said; "Are you hiring?"

It was an awkward moment I have to say, but all worth the cause and reasoning. Let's just say that all is well with the encounter and I am currently doing an internship-based position with the opportunity to hire. The chances of this happening without direct experience and an education is slim to none and for God to bring the job to me is more than words can say. I wanted to share this experience with you in hopes of displaying another example of the power of God. It seems that once I had put my total trust in the Lord, he was more than willing to show me his glory.

CHAPTER 12:
DARKNESS BEHIND THE
NEW AGE MOVEMENT

"...for prophecy never came by the will of man, but holy men of God spoke as
they were moved by the Holy Spirit."
(2 PETER 1:21)

This painful experience gave me a tremendous amount of awareness and realization that mankind has grown way too confident with what they think they can do with the spirit world and its supernatural powers. It is baffling for me to see how we as humans, not all, have come to terms with the belief that they can not only control but prophesize their own destiny and existence. Realistically, this is solely a reflection of one's impatience and ignorance towards God's timing and purpose. Since the beginning of time people have been practicing sorcery, worshiping idols, and playing marvel either by practicing mediumship or through the seeking of psychics and mediums, which by the way is forbidden under God's law.

Spiritualism has been identified as the trickery of the evil one since the beginning of time. If we are not serving God, we are serving Satan and his legions of demons. I'm not sure where we went wrong with believing that it is okay to summon spiritual beings out in the open, but I believe that the explosive phenomena started spiraling out of control once the western world got a hold of the occult, which according to history, was around the 1970's and 1980's.

Its roots are traced to a multitude of sources, such as, Hinduism, gnostic traditions, astrology, spiritualism, channeling, shamanism, Wicca, neo-pagan traditions, etc. In my opinion, this is a fabricated worship directly controlled by the evil one, also known as the devil whom we all know is God's direct enemy. The affiliation ultimately gives people the option to shop for beliefs and practices that are solely tailored to one's own selfish wants and needs. I didn't see it as such prior to my conversion, but since my baptism my perception of this reality is now evidently understood through the flow of divine knowledge that now undeniably seeps through my veins.

There are thousands of books out there that not only teach but claim that we can not only manifest our desires but also control and alter our already pre-determined future, all with the help of ancestral spirits and other spiritual forces. It has been written since BC (Before Christ) of the existence of evil angels and how they actively roam the earth in a very deceitful manner. Satan or the Devil, whatever you want to call him, masquerades as an angel of light. His servants (legions of demons) also disguise themselves as servants of righteousness. *(2 Corinthians 11:14-15)*

It can simply start with an innocent interest in the power of crystals, astrology, numerology, energy healing and transducent deep meditations. These practices claim to help calm the calamities within our spiritual well-being but what its actually doing is opening the closed spaces in the psyche mind and giving an invitation and legal ground for demons to dwell in. Whether you realize it or not, what your actually doing is flagging down evil spirits and directly giving them permission to interact with you. Why such evil is allowed to exist among us and have the power to subconsciously influence our mind in a heinous way is still a mystery. I pondered on that question quite often and it wasn't until a little later that I would get the answer through a vision.

Since when did the Bible reverse these facts and warnings? In spite of this, people continue to call on these evil angels, the same ones that we have been warned about since the beginning of time. These ancient enemies of God have not changed their evil place and or purpose on earth and I'm pretty sure they don't have any plans to do so in the future. There is good reason as to why God banned Lucifer and his followers from heaven, and if one continues to be in alliance with their powers, that same person is also supporting their defiance towards God, our creator. Psychics and mediums unfortunately fall victim to the illusions of the devil's lies by being made to believe that they are unique and gifted not realizing that they are actually signing over their rights from everlasting life. I also know from personal experience and by talking to other psychics that we feel the need to share our gift in hopes of helping others with their personal struggles by providing answers otherwise unknown.

On the other hand, I have also come across psychics that are fake and deceitful, and scam victims out of their money out of pure greed. I, on the other hand, always did my work out of pure heart and sincere compassion and would not charge a fee most of the time. I rightly believe that God saw the integrity in my heart and knew that I was honestly lost in the works of the devil, and because of my innocence, he mercifully decided to shed the light behind the veil.

I now firmly believe that spiritualists after a while become lost in translation once the devil has successfully deceived them into thinking that the only darkness that exists is the one here on earth. Psychics and mediums refer to this darkness as low vibrational energies, negative entities and or earthbound spirits. The devil deceives his victims by supplying them with incredible insight and psychic information that others, such as myself, feel compelled to share. In return, we become obliged with the fascination that we need to utilize this gift in order to help others. Furthermore, Satan falsely makes the person of interest (victim) believe that he or she is special to the spirit world and that their gift is desperately needed to help heal the world and the people in it. At some point the victim ultimately ends up biting the bait and surrendering to this sham life, which they now believe is a life calling.

Satan is an intelligent fallen angel and was originally created by the very same God that created us. He is going to know what your family members look like, what their nicknames are and the specific details of their life. He knows the ins and outs of your deepest desires including what you had for dinner last night and what vacations you will be taking in the future. He can very easily disguise himself as an angel of light and or a deceased love one with no problem. This powerful display of deceit is what tricks humans to believe that they are channeling their loved ones but in reality, are communicating with legions of demons. To put it simply, God's enemy and his character is the same big bad wolf that is portrayed in the legendary fairy tale story also known as *The Little Red Riding Hood*.

The devil is very jealous of God's love towards the human race and will do everything in his power to deter you from receiving the gift of an everlasting life and yet here we are 3,000 years later, still falling to the traps of the fallen one. Spiritualism falsely teaches us that there is no hell and tricks us into thinking that we are all going into the light and that we are all connected in a form called vibrational energy. Seriously? I highly doubt that I will be in the same boat of light as Saddam Hussein and or Hitler. Besides, I was shown a quick glimpse of hell, and it wasn't pretty.

The spiritualistic occult also encourages us to act freely without owning up to our debt, called sin. It puffs us up with human ego and as a result we start feeling entitled to it all. Spiritualistic practitioners do believe in a Jesus, but rather in a modern-day Jesus, not the true resurrected Jesus. In their view, Jesus is an ascended master believed to have been a spiritually enlightened being who in past incarnations was an ordinary human, who underwent a series of spiritual transformations originally called initiations. He is included with several other ascended masters who supposedly sits on a cosmic pyramid, so they say. The term ascended master is referred to a being, who through his spiritual work, raised his consciousness and vibration to such a level where he was able to complete his or her karma and attain "God realization." Really?

These irrational teachings are made up by a bunch of philosophers and is not taught in the true holy scriptures of the bible. People tend to make stuff up in hopes of trying to get answers to the meaning of life and this analyzation is just a small piece of their belief system.

Either way, you cannot practice spiritualism and believe in the teachings of the bible at the same time. It would be condescending to do so, yet there are many Christians that still seek psychic readings from time to time. Consulting mediums is like committing adultery against the one true God. You cannot expect to attain everlasting life from God and continue to stay acquainted with his mortal enemy. This goes back to our original ancestors, Adam and Eve, who were also deceived in the very same manner. His tactics haven't changed, it is still very much the same and will remain that way until his time of condemnation.

People lose hope in the creator for many reasons, mainly due to the many pains and strains of life. In reality, we were born into sin, including the enemy that caused it. We are part of the story of evil which means that as long as we exist here on earth, we will always experience the cavalry that comes with it. However, there is hope and how beautiful is it to know that even after all this, God is still holding his promise to the covenant and the reconciliation that he has mercifully put in place with mankind. Even though Adam and Eve permanently strained our relationship with God, he obviously still holds an immense amount of love for us, in fact he adores his creation and that is why he came up with a rescue plan, which is clearly revealed in the Holy Bible.

Because of the witnessing of my revelation, a few of my friends have returned to God's salvation or at least have drawn closer to him. My family was also deeply affected by what they saw unfold, which bought about my son's baptism, my daughter's attendance at church and even my husband, who has been a skeptic all his life and is now also a believer of Christ. The biggest shock of all came when my mother, who has been an atheist all her life, also decided to give God a chance after presenting all the evidence. I hope and pray that there will be many other souls saved as a result. I wholeheartedly encourage you to use my example as a tone to set for others which I pray will prevent another soul from being lost in the perilous journey of darkness.

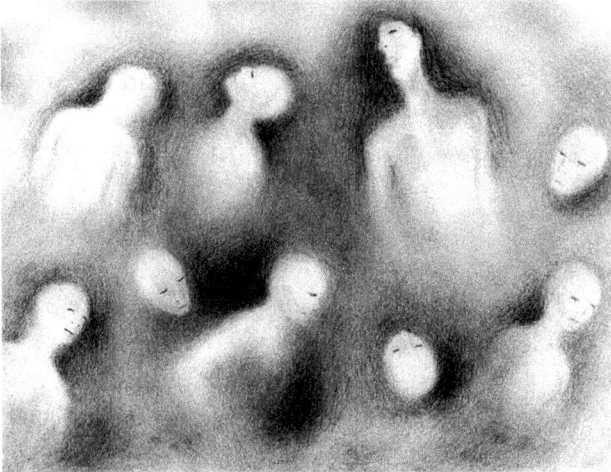

CHAPTER 13:
SAINT PETER REVEALED

"...that you may be mindful of the words which were spoken before by the holy prophets, and of the commandment of us, the apostles of the Lord and Savior."
(2 PETER 3:2)

In the summer of 2018 Saint Peter graciously revealed himself to me during a divine encounter which would ultimately lead me to paint this portrait of him.

Before judging, please take into account that I have no previous experience and or training in the field of arts and know that I did my best to portray his appearance in this painting.

I stood in the entrance of a doorway in a room that was filled with a warm bright yellowish gold luminesces and was bright all around. I immediately noticed a woman sitting to my left with a bunch of empty chairs around her. Her hair was blonde, wavy and medium length.

Once she noticed my presence, she looked directly at me with a smile and said, "Are you ready to meet him?"

I replied by asking her; "Ready to meet who?"

She then said; "Saint Peter of course."

I was immediately overcome by an intense feeling of excitement and recall thinking, no way, am I seriously going to meet Saint Peter? I am really going to meet Saint Peter. I looked straight ahead then over to my right and noticed another entrance way with an even brighter glow. Feeling overwhelmed with anticipation I became aware of my shallow breathing sounds and rapid palpitations. A tall man suddenly appeared in the doorway whom was dressed in a black priest robe with a white collar that featured an embroider pattern consistent with small white crosses that distinctly traveled down the center of his robe and all the way down to the rim of his cloak.

The black gown flowed freely and I noticed that there wasn't a belt or a rope of any kind around the waist. He stood there with a confident stance and I couldn't help but to notice his undeniable warm smile and loving stare. He appeared to be in his 30's with light brown skin tone and dark brown eyes and his nose was flat and wide.

Then without physically speaking he said the following telepathically, *"Hello Beatrix, I am very proud of what you have accomplished. "Fear no more for I am with you always"*

Then I suddenly awoke, I looked at the clock and noticed that it was only 2:00 am. Feeling emotional and weepy from the experience I now had this very strong urge to cry, and not in a soft quiet state but rather in an uncontrollable hysterical manner.

Because I didn't want to wake my husband up, I hurried to the bathroom and wept myself out until there were no more tears to dry. The next morning, I couldn't wait to tell my husband of what had happened and the encounter I experienced. He was groggy upon awakening of course and before I could finish up with the details of what I had encountered, I started crying again but this time with tears of joy. This revelation had such a huge impact on my spiritual well-being and left me in a state of euphoria for the rest of that weekend.

The following Monday I planned on sharing my experience with a couple of co-workers, especially to those that knew of my gift and have done readings on before.

As soon as I got to work that Monday the first thing I did was boast about my experience to an employee that wasn't a strong believer in Christ. I went over the details of my experience and didn't get much of a response, which was expected.

As I walked away to call in the first scheduled patient, I looked at one of my co-workers one more time and said, "I am telling you, I met Saint Peter."

I grabbed the first chart of the day and proceeded to get the work day going. I usually don't look at the name on the charts until I am ready to call the patient in, what happened next would seal the deal with my Saint Peter experience.

Taking a quick glance at the bottom tab of the manila chart I was astounded to learn that the patient's last name was St. Peter, with that exact spelling. I couldn't believe my eyes and for a second, I thought that I was imagining things because I was still on cloud nine from my weekend experience. I felt paralyzed and paused for a second before calling the patient in so I could gather my thoughts of what was taking place. I let out a small giggle of joy and bought the patient in quickly and before notifying the medical doctor of her first patient, I showed my co-worker the chart. She seemed amused and perplexed by the phenomenal occurrence and reacted to the happening by saying, *"Only you Bea, it only happens to you."* She couldn't comprehend the extraordinary experience, but I knew otherwise.

I felt a need to share this part of the story as I believe it was a continuation of Saint Peter's revelation and he wanted to assure me that what I experienced with him over that weekend was in fact real and true. I have never come across a last name like this before and the chances of it happening again is small to none.

Saint Peter was martyred 2,000 years ago, yet he still continues to exist in a heavenly place as of this day. This is an extraordinary confirmation, proving that if you follow Jesus, like Peter did, eternal life will be given to you as promised. I have been blessed beyond compare to have such a divine encounter and will be forever grateful for him taking his time to make his presence known to a quiet girl, such as myself, who is not much known to others. I will forever praise him in the highest for he not only intervened in my salvation but also guided me back to the one true God.

I am now very aware and accept our one true God and creator and I am especially fond of Jesus Christ, our redeemer. Saint Peter will also have a special place in my heart, how could he not be after all that he has done. I actually have a wooden plaque with his image imprinted, which sits on my nightstand by my bed to this very day. It is not the first time a saint has appeared to us here on earth, but just one of many. Saint Peter stayed faithful to his discipleship role (according to scripture) after Jesus's death and preached to the lands and its people until his very last breath as a martyr. I truly believe that he is still continuing to lead the lost, just like he did when he was alive, except this time he leads from the heavens above.

I am not here to judge other cultures or the multitude of religions that exist today, that is not what this book is about. I am simply here to testify and to be a witness to the existence of Satan and his demons and the power of God's authority to the skeptics and other psychic mediums. Earlier in the book I gave detailed accounts of my experiences with a handful of religions that I have studied and entangled myself with but never really surrendered myself fully. Not only have I been shown the truth by supernatural experiences and manifestations but the veil has also been fully lifted and the light has finally reached my heart. There are plenty of other books that attempt to prove the existence of heaven and hell yet people still refuse the fact and disregard the evidence. I don't know how God will use my story because there are many other books similar to mine, but he obviously has plans beyond my comprehension. I am simply following his command and trusting his plans on how he will utilize me for his glory.

CHAPTER 14:
JESUS CHRIST

"I am the Way, the Truth, and the Life. No one comes to the Father except through me."
(JOHN 14:6)

A vision of Jesus and the painting that followed.

On December 10th of 2018, I was given a vision where I believe I caught a glimpse of Jesus Christ, whom I know to be our lord and savior. In the vision, I was screaming Jesus's name for reasons unknown when suddenly I noticed a wall in front of me which seemed to resemble an old mason stone wall with a window in the center. I walked up to the window and peeked out in a sneaky manner because for some reason or another I didn't want to be seen. Once I caught glimpse of the outside, I pulled back quickly because the light that was emitting was way too bright for my eyes to see. I peeked once again and this time I noticed that there was a man in a white gown who was walking around in an authoritative but loving manner. I got the feeling that he was watching over his people and guarding them. His gown was whiter than white and it seemed to flow beautifully and in sync. The sleeve of the gown was long and I couldn't make out the location of his hands. His hair was wavy and highlighted with the colors of brown.

The vision was suddenly disrupted and although I was now awake, I still seemed to be in a transient state and was still very sleepy. As I dosed back to sleep, I heard a mother crying and screaming, "*not my baby, not my baby*" Instantly I thought of mother Mary and knew that what was being portrayed was her screams when Jesus was being crucified. I then saw two pairs of feet that were not only shackled but restrained while walking up a hill. The chains were extremely rusted and made out of cast iron.

Next, I saw a huge wooden cross being dragged on a dirt and dusty road. At that moment, I heard a male voice say, "*nine-inch nails.*" I then saw two legs dangling on a cross and the feet placed in an inverted position. Being fully aware of what was happening, I continued to allow the information to flow through. Subsequently, I saw a huge mallet that specifically resembled the hammer from the movie "Thor." The person that was sledge hammering the cross appeared to be wearing a cape of some sort and was very fit and muscular. What I saw next might be controversial to others but I am not going to edit my vision for one's own liking. The nails appeared to have been placed in the peroneus brevis part of the lower shin, in other words, not through the feet but rather through the sides of his lower leg.

I now believe that my vision of Jesus and the experience that directly followed was simply a confirmation to my skepticism and fear.

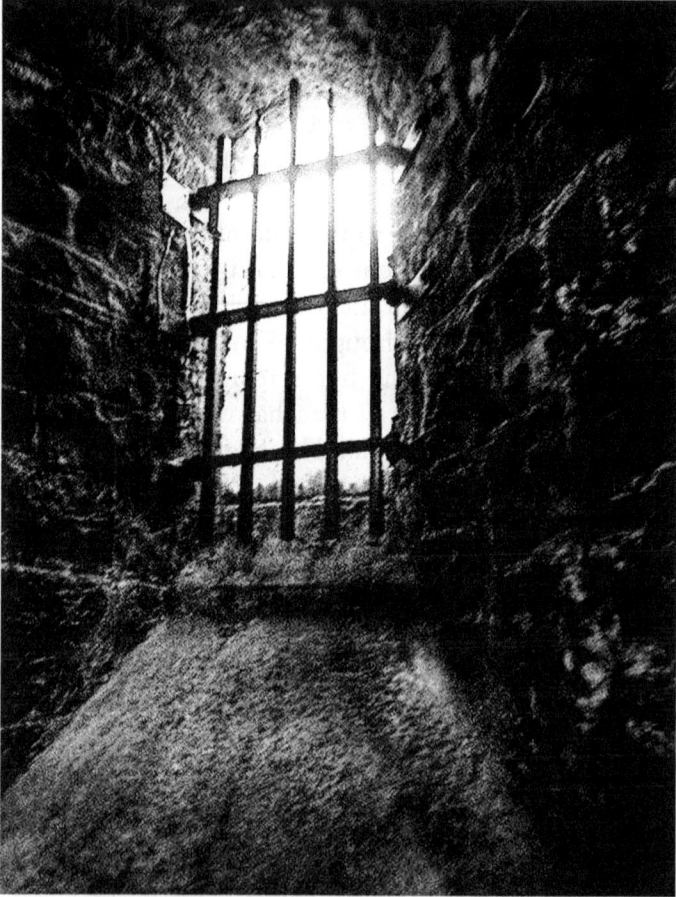

A representation of the visionary place where I saw Jesus from.

CHAPTER 15:
NOAH AND THE ARK

I have to be honest and freely admit that until my recent vision of Noah, I really didn't give much thought to the story of Noah's Ark and the great flood. Most people have heard about the legends of this great flood most likely through bible studies and or movies. A lot of people are skeptic about the famous revelation and its relevance but the story still remains high profile in the biblical chapters of Genesis. If you haven't heard of the miraculous boat and Noah's calling, here is a quick synopsis according to the bible.

According to scripture, Noah was a righteous man, blameless among the people of his time, and he walked faithfully with God. Noah had three sons: Shem, Ham and Japheth.

At this time the earth was corrupt in God's sight and was full of violence. God saw how corrupt the earth had become, for all the people on earth had corrupted their ways. God said to Noah:

I am going to put an end to all people, for the earth is filled with violence because of them. I am surely going to destroy both them and the earth. Make yourself an ark made of cypress wood; make rooms in it and coat it with pitch inside and out. This is how you are to build it: The ark is to be three hundred cubits long, fifty cubits wide and thirty cubits high. Make a roof for it, leaving below the roof an opening one cubit high all around. Put a door in the side of the ark and make a lower, middle and upper deck.

I am going to bring floodwaters on the earth to destroy all life under the heavens, and every creature that has the breath of life in it. Everything on earth will perish. But I will establish my covenant with you, and you will enter the ark—you and your sons and your wife and your sons' wives with you. You are to bring into the ark two of all living creatures, male and female, to keep them alive with you. Two of every kind of bird, of every kind of animal and of every kind of creature that moves along the ground will come to you to be kept alive. You are to take every kind of food that is to be eaten and store it away as food for you and for them.

Noah did all that the Lord commanded him and survived the flooded earth that took place for a hundred and fifty days. After the flood Noah lived 350 years and lived a total of 950 years, and then he died according to scripture. (Genesis chapters 6-9)

I am still baffled by my vision of Noah and feel honored to have been shown his biblical existence. I tried my hardest to portray his appearance in my drawing, and actually got pretty caught up with perfecting his features. A week after my vision I debated back and forth with myself whether or not I should try sketching the great Noah but was reluctant to put him on paper, that is until God decided to make a point for me to do so.

I can't recall the exact day but I do remember that it was more towards the end of the week, possibly on a Thursday, when the Lord called unto me and basically said, *you must draw Noah and include him in your book.*

It was around 2:30 am in the morning and for some reason I suddenly became wide awake and alert and couldn't fall back asleep. I decided to scroll my Facebook page, which I usually do when I want to make myself tired again. It didn't take long for me to get drowsy again and before I could drift off to sleep a sudden vision of an unfamiliar face randomly appeared to me. The first thing that caught my attention was his bright pastel blue colored eyes and his unusual high cheekbones. His nose was small and pointing upwards and I could see his nostrils. This face just sat there blinking and staring at me. I tried to pull myself out of the engagement and succeeded but not before seeing another vision of an old man with an unsteady balance wobbling back and forth. His hair was quite long, white and brittle. He had a slight hunch to his stance yet his calf muscles appeared bulky and strong.

Out of fear I sat up immediately to try to get myself awake and alert. At this point I still didn't know who the projected vision was and whether it was good or evil. I immediately said a prayer and headed downstairs to the kitchen to get a drink of water. I tried to dismiss the incident but also felt compelled to acknowledge it because I knew that it had some sort of important significance. I went back upstairs and laid back down in an attempt to fall back asleep. I was now at ease and felt safe enough to fall back asleep again. I said another quick prayer and as I starting dosing off to sleep, I heard a loving but commanding voice say in my head *"Noah the drunk."*

That morning, upon awakening, the first thought that popped into my head was Noah and the flood. As I went about my morning routine the word "Norwegian" and "Neanderthal" kept crossing my mind.

My son got on the school bus as usual, I took the dogs out, made sure all the lights were turned off and walked out the door. I jumped in the car, put my car in reverse and backed down my driveway and onto the street but before shifting the car into drive I felt this sudden urge to look up at the sky. What I saw next not only blew my mind but also left me in a state of joy for the rest of the day. I saw an extremely beautiful colorful arching rainbow peeking through the clouds, it was perfect in shape and extraordinarily long in length. The colors were vivid and bright and the layer of colors seemed to lay perfectly and in synch with one another. I quickly slammed my breaks on and started gazing at this magnificent rainbow for a few minutes. I couldn't help but to smile at the occurrence because I knew that this wasn't just an ordinary rainbow laid out before me. During my ride to work it suddenly dawned on me that the rainbow was a huge significance in Noah's story, according to scripture. In the bible it is written that when Noah and his family came out of the ark, the first thing they did was offer a gift of thanks to God. Then God gave them a rainbow in the sky as a sign and a reminder of his promise to Noah and his family.

For the next couple of weeks, I couldn't get Noah and the word Norwegian out of my head. God was constantly reminding me of my vision almost on a daily basis. I was obviously being ushered by the divine and the holy spirit to draw my vision and the experience. Between license plates, social media, advertisements and daily conversations, I couldn't escape Noah's name, that is until I surrendered myself to God's instruction. God obviously has a comical side to him because his serendipity moments have given me many chuckles along the way.

Once I started working on Noah's portrait, I was given another visual perception and this time it was a quick glimpse of the boat. The boat was shaped in a geometrical manner which reminded me of an octagon shaped stop sign. I don't know if that was the top part of the boat, but it sure seemed as such. In the image I was looking down on the boat from up above and the projection of the boat appeared to be in the midst of when it was being built. I also saw a woman carrying plywood in her arms while climbing up a set of spiral stairs. The steps seemed to be unusually long in relationship to its width and I especially noticed that the stairs stemmed centrally within the boat and the stairs did not have any railings attached. The woman appeared to be older in age and her apparel consisted of a heavy-set dress made out of wool. There was some sort of a belt that was fastened around her wide hips. Her shoes were flat and reached all the way up to her ankles. The shoes were made out of pig hide skin and the wool shoelaces intertwined in a jagged fashion through the loop holes.

There were hundreds of wooden beams and lumbar material scattered all around on the floor of the boat and I took an immediate notice to the many mismatched wood colorings. I was then jolted out of the visionary dream and as I laid there in silence with my eyes closed, I heard gurgling water sounds followed by oceanic sound waves. I then saw a gigantic body of water closing in on me rapidly and I suddenly felt like I was drowning. I forced myself to awake out of fear and tried to make sense of what I just experienced. While lying there stunned and dumbfounded I quickly came to the conclusion that God was confirming Noah's story to me. I fell back asleep and when I awoke in the morning the first thought that came to my mind was me needing to get all this information down on paper.

In the midst of sketching Noah, I went through at least 50 sheets of paper. I felt inadequate to be able to perform such a task. As it came closer to finishing my so-called work of art, precisely on the day I finished, I was given more specific detailed thoughts about the environment and the type of food and water they survived on. Cabbage was used as a meal source quite often and so was goats' milk. I also saw a wooden beam with stored dried herbs hanging upside down. Dandelions and some sort of roots that resembled a barley root. Wheat was another item that was accessorized on their food chain. I started smelling fire smoke during this experience and was shown a small fire pit, which they used to keep warm and was used as a source of light during night fall. In my vision, I distinctively saw five people praying and holding hands around the fire.

I tried my best to sketch and draw Noah the exact same way I saw him but again, I am not an artist nor a painter. My goal is to get the reader to see and understand of how God has communicated such important information to me and to hopefully have the reader accept the fact that Noah's story is in fact tried and true. It is obvious that I have a gift, a gift that I will never again use in an evil manner. If it goes against scripture and the biblical truth, I want absolutely nothing to do with it. Why the Lord decided to reveal Noah to me is beyond my comprehension and still humbles me to this day. I have confidently come to the understanding that once I truly surrendered myself to the Lord, he reached out and revealed himself to me.

My Vision of Noah

CHAPTER 16:
DIVINE MESSAGES

I would like to share some of the visions that I experienced during my recovery phase and reformatory period. I believe that it's important to share this part of my experience because it played a huge role in confirming the authenticity of the bible. I will not be able to give the exact dates and times that these all occurred on but that shouldn't affect the perception or the relevance of the insights I was graciously given.

One of the most significant visions that affected me the most was of the bible. The image appeared like a computer screen projection that floated in the air and stood about 3 feet in front of me. The bible was opened and was about three times bigger than its original size. I then saw a hand come down and stamp the bible. The bible image then focused in closer and then I saw the bible being stamped again with what appeared to be an old vintage red wax stamp. The image then disappeared and I immediately grabbed my phone and looked up vintage stamping because that is what it reminded me of. I discovered that this particular stamping style served as a stamp of indisputable authenticity, just as a signature is accepted in the world today.

The use of seals can be traced back to the old Testament, where it mentions that Jezebel used Ahab's seal to counterfeit important documents. In a time when many were illiterate, they were used in place of a signature to authenticate agreements, contracts, wills and letters, which conferred rights and privileges and basically executed acts in someone's name. God was in essence telling me that the contents of the bible is authentic and true. This image continues to linger with me today, especially when someone challenges the bible's truth.

Virgin Mary

Not long ago, on a typical day, I was going about my daily business and my work shift was coming to a close. I clocked out and felt excited about going to see my horses. While driving in route, out of the blue, I started thinking about mother Mary, her role in our salvation and whether she was really a virgin. Yes, it's true, I still struggled with the idea at times. I was pondering on thoughts about the fear and heartache she must have experienced during her lifetime. As I turned onto the driveway where the horse's stalls stood, I suddenly heard a loving male voice say *"She was my surrogate Bea, a virgin pure in heart."* I froze in fear but that fear dissipated pretty quickly once I realized that God was confirming my doubts about Mary's virginity. Then I further heard *"She was fifteen when I placed your savior in her womb, you will see her in heaven in her special castle."*

I remember driving home anxious with excitement because I couldn't wait to tell my husband about my new revelation. After that divine message I never questioned God about Mary's authenticity. To be perfectly honest, a lot of people have trouble comprehending and believing Mary's virginity, including myself. Since the beginning I never questioned Jesus and his existence, only the Virgin Mary posed questions in my mind.

Adam and Eve

It was the middle of the week and the usual mundane day was coming to a close. I wrapped up my nightly chores and although I was quite tired, I still couldn't get myself to fall asleep. I decided to start counting sheep in hopes of cutting all the noise off from the world. I started dosing off but before I could fully fall into a deep sleep God decided to give me another divine message. I was shown two beautiful beings, a male and a female. They were both naked and very majestic and basically flawless. Without hesitation, I immediately thought to myself, wow look how beautiful Adam and Eve was, I don't know how I knew but I just knew who they were. Then a huge red heart appeared before me and it was placed directly in front of them.

I suddenly felt an overwhelming sense of pure love, as if the creation was my own making and although my eyes were closed, that didn't stop the tears from rolling down my face. I am pretty confident in the notion that for a second God was letting me feel his love and power towards mankind. What he showed me next helped me understand the reasons of why we have been left to endure the struggles of life since the beginning of time.

The red heart that was placed in front of Adam and Eve slowly started cracking in half, straight down the middle. The Lord was displaying the intense devastation he felt when his first human creations fell to sin and how we broke his heart in the process. Mercifully he has come up with a rescue plan but to this day we are still prisoners to that repercussion. It only took 43 years for me to truly come to love the meaning of the word "merciful" but it's better to be late rather than never.

God Wants Me To Go To Church

One particular Sunday I awoke around 5:30 am, although my alarm was set for 7:30 am. I took the dogs out for a potty run but for some reason I didn't have much motivation left to do anything else that morning. Feeling fatigued, I made the quick decision to skip church that morning and laid back down in bed. I laid down on my back with my body facing up although I usually don't sleep in that position because I have a tendency to snore really loud. As I laid there still contemplating whether or not to go to church, I ended up falling back asleep. My sleep was quickly interrupted by an experience that was initiated by the Lord above which of course quickly prompted me to change my mind about not wanting to go to church.

In the vision, I was shown a cross that was covered in blood stains. I then saw a huge paintbrush of some sort which was drenched in blood. Next, I saw an extremely large hand grab the brush, then the blood drenched brush splattered me with such intensity that it woke me out of the sleep.

Once awake, I heard a male gentle voice in my head say , *"Remission of sin"* followed by, *"Freedom."*

I knew all too well by now what that meant and understood that I needed to keep going to church to take communion so I can continuously be cleansed from sin. As you can guess, I made it to that morning Sunday service and even arrived fifteen minutes early.

Spoken For

Winter was dragging and it was still early February. I was still having some issues with memories of my past and at times I would find myself unsure of God's forgiveness even after being baptized and reformed.

The devil loves to feed your fear and anxiety and during this particular experience, I am pretty sure that the ruler of all evil was having a ball with my feelings of doubt and regret. Throughout this particular day I noticed that I was having random onsets of intense emotional moments, especially when a certain part of my past would pop into my head. I was pondering about my disappointments more than usual and by the end of the day I felt exhausted by my constant fretting. We're human and we all tend to have good and bad emotional instances, but on this particular day my heart seemed heavy with remorse. I had just finished feeding my horses and because the temperature was below zero I did as little as possible with aspects to cleaning the stalls and couldn't wait to get back in the car.

Once inside the car I took a few minutes to warm up and decided to say a repentance prayer out loud. During the prayer I started to feel an overwhelming sense of grief and ended up shedding a few tears as a result. Honestly, I felt emotionally and mentally beat up from that day and felt spiritually deprived overall. I put my car in reverse and as I started to drive away, I remember saying to myself, *"I hope God can forgive my doubtful and weak moments."*

Following that thought I received the following message: *"I forgive you my child and you have been spoken for; your name is in the book of life."*

Instantaneously, I thought to myself, *Oh my God, the book of life really does exist?* I've heard about it a few times throughout my life but never really gave it much thought, until now. This was a huge revelation for me, I mean huge and I felt relieved knowing that I was counted for.

My doubt and fear instantly dissipated and a sense of peace overcame my body. Since the experience I no longer let my fear and doubt control me in such depths.

Perfecting the Soul

I have been suffering with chronic bladder pain for a couple of months and on this particular day the flare and the pain was very intense. I took an aspirin in the morning but that didn't ease the pain much. I had a couple of appointments scheduled that day including a parent teacher conference meeting. I made these commitments a few months back and couldn't cancel because it would take months to get another appointment. The parent teacher conference didn't go very well and the doctor's appointment ended up being canceled because the provider I was scheduled to see was on call that week and he had a couple of emergency surgery cases to attend to.

The day was not going well and by 4:00 pm the pain was getting to me psychologically. Feeling defeated and frustrated I decided to try to lay down for a nap. I was desperate to feel pain free and I went into a deep prayer mode. I was begging God to give me strength to bare the pain and was questioning the existence of suffering. I was trying to compromise with our maker and felt as though he was ignoring my begging. I thought to myself, there are millions of people out there suffering way more than me and here I was complaining about my stupid bladder pains.

After I finished praying, I chose to take a warm bath rather than a nap because the pain would have prevented me from falling asleep anyway. In the tub I tried to use a breathing technique that pregnant people usually use when they are in labor, but no avail. I just couldn't get over the suffering and out of frustration I looked up at the bathroom ceiling and just kept asking God to make it stop. He seemed to stay silent with aspects to my plea and by this time I ran out of words to pray. I stepped out of the tub and proceeded to dry myself off but I couldn't find the towel. I decided to make a run to my bedroom across the hall and hoped that nobody would catch a glimpse of me naked.

I grabbed the towel, wrapped myself up with it tightly and slowly made my way to the bed. I sat there in silence for a few minutes and before I laid my head down, I got the answer that I was deeply pondering upon.

I was told the following; *"My dear child, the suffering that you endure will perfect your soul before the eyes of the father so that you may relinquish your rights into heaven."*

This was deep, and I am sure that this meaning will have differential meanings for many different people at many various levels, I will leave it at that.

Hall of Shame

This divine message came to me in a dream that would ultimately confirm my belief about demons. In the dream, I was standing in front of this huge black building and I had a sense that whatever was in the building was not good in nature. The sky was dark and gray and the area seemed secluded.

As I took a closer look, I noticed that there were large white capitalized letters engraved on the building. The writing on the left side of the building said "FALLEN ANGELS" and the writing on the right side said "HALL OF SHAME."

Suddenly a middle-eastern looking man appeared to the left of me and introduced himself by saying, "I am from Syria."

I replied and said, "Hello," and nothing else.

We were now both looking at the building in front of us. I felt awkward with his presence but knew he had something to tell me.

He said, "You must never enter that building no matter what the cost, do you understand?"

I replied and said, "Okay, but why not?"

Then he said, "That building consists of dark angels and they all worship the master of illusions"

I asked what he met by that and he said, "They obey Lucifer and the root of sin and you must not omit to their faulty presence"

He then disappeared in an instant and I was left thinking that I needed to run for my life and quickly as possible at best.

I wanted to share these experiences in my book so I could provide the reader with some examples of how God can communicate with his human creations. I have had many other visions, but that would entail writing another book.

You Will Not Be Forgotten

This particular dream vision took place on a Tuesday afternoon around 3:30 p.m. The day was hot and muggy and I wanted nothing to do with the 99-degree weather that was sweltering outside. My eyes were tired and I was barely able to keep my eyes open during my drive home from work. As soon as I got home, I changed into comfortable clothing and laid down for what I thought would be a refreshing nap. I fell asleep pretty quickly only to wake up in a strange and unfamiliar home.

I attempted to stand up but I seemed to be stuck where I was laying. I immediately knew that this was going to be a supernatural encounter. I tried hard to release myself from whatever was holding me back but to no avail. I then felt an old familiar creepy feeling, the one that I always used to get before an evil presence would appear. A large, tall, red demonic figure appeared in the corner of the room by the doorway.

I said to myself, *Why is this happening again?*

But there was something different about this occurrence because for some reason I didn't feel petrified or helpless like I use to before. Even though I couldn't get up, I immediately started saying the Lord's Prayer. The entity disappeared and I was suddenly free to roam the unfamiliar home I was in. I attempted to chase after the demon, but in a flying manner. I was floating around the house when I suddenly felt the demon's presence behind me, once again it was trying to oppress me.

I said, *"I'm not afraid of you, you son of a bitch!"* Yes, I said it just like that.

I felt this rage inside me and I yelled out the following; *"I adore my father above and so will you"* I then said, *"You will worship the Lord above and bow before the almighty God."*

Then the demon replied and said, "I will do what I want and will not adore anything or anyone if I don't want to." I was lost for words, I didn't even know what I was commanding; I have never said or knew of such words of intelligence like this before. I started to panic and so I immediately started yelling for Jesus to come and help me.

I was desperately looking for a way out and even tried to force myself to awake but I was stuck with no place to hide. I started screaming, "Father please help me, where are you? I can't see you, where are you?"

I started sobbing like a baby because I left like I was forced to fend off an evil spirit, once again, without any help from God.

Suddenly I heard a high-pitched singing voice coming towards me. I remember thinking, wow, it sounds like an orchestra coming down the hall.

At once, I was propelled in an upward fashion, towards the ceiling, through the walls and into the sky. It was very quick and direct. The singing now become very loud and prominent, and the pitch altered into a high vibrational ringing tone. I reached my hands into the darkness and noticed that my hands were now glowing. I felt safe and comforted, I knew that I was being rescued by angels and immediately submitted myself to their taking.

Then in the midst of the darkness a beautiful glowing light appeared. It is hard to describe the colors because it is something that

I have never seen before, but I will try my best. The aura of colors included dark sparkling purple with a gold hue, green emerald in the middle and yellowish tones mixed in with an intense white light around its orb. The shape was asymmetrical and it seemed to move in a circular motion like a wheel, which appeared to be three dimensional.

I felt myself starting to cry again and even had trouble catching my breath. The angels then said, *"There is no need to worry, you won't be forgotten, you will be remembered at the time of transition."* I can't even describe how relieved I felt at that moment.

I was then allowed to fly freely again when, unexpectedly, I was placed in this beautiful green fortress. It looked like earth but one hundred times better. The trees were vibrantly green, the ferns were gigantic and the air seemed light and crisp. The daylight was brighter than ever and the environment felt clean and safe.

I saw houses all around, some were made out of glass. It was breathtaking and I felt no worry or pain in the moment. I was then placed in one of the glass houses. The trimming was gold and from inside I could see everything around me. The view was crystal clear and the fortress felt like my home. I turned to see what was behind me and I saw these two reclined chairs that were made of pure gold. They seemed very elongated and I seemed to know that they were stationed tightly to the floor of the home. It looked very futuristic and it actually reminded me of the Star Trek Voyager television series, the enterprise and its commander center chair. I interpreted the meaning of the chairs as a place of rest.

I finally awoke but had a very hard time trying to keep my eyes open. My body felt heavy and I felt like I had been physically battered. I looked over to the clock and realized that I only slept for about thirty-five minutes, although it felt like an eternity. It took me a good twenty minutes to get my body out of bed and when I finally did, I walked like a drunk who was out partying the night before. I swayed my way to the bathroom in an attempt to wash my face with cold water, but that in itself took a good ten minutes. I was in a trance and it hurt just to think.

I then heard that loving command voice in my head again, and he said, *"Turn your Microsoft on and record your vision."* I knew exactly what that meant and by the evening the task was complete.

CHAPTER 17:
NEW CONVICTION

After being dragged through the pits, chewed up and spit out, God still wanted me. Even though I was broken and scarred, he still decided to forgive my nonsense and use me for his glory. It has been an extremely difficult transformational journey as you can see but the pain has been worth it. It took an intense amount of healing to be able to admit to such a conclusion but I can actually say now that I am thankful for the scars. I don't think that I would have been able to truly come to know God's heart without my obliviousness and his mercy.

Who wouldn't want to be pardoned for their mistakes and transgressions? I am sure that even atheists yearn for some sort of acceptance and reconciliation deep down inside, although they might not admit it publicly, I can assure you that those feelings have been experienced in silence. Each and every one of us is born with a deep desire to be loved unconditionally and to be forgiven mercifully, this includes the believers and the non-believers. Its imprinted in our DNA and there is absolutely no way around it.

There are many different deep-rooted reasons of why people choose to turn away from the God almighty. Whatever the reasoning is, it won't change the fact that we were created by the Lord above. We were born into sin, therefore, suffering from sinful acts that are inflicted upon one another. Many times, this can entail very painful trials and tribulations for others but staying mad at God will not resolve the pain and the losses we incur as a result. We don't have the antidote for the human condition, only God does.

I believe that these trials are a preparation to season and mature the soul for reasons God only knows. A lot of people get blind-sided by the sorrow and resentment and understandably so, but how unfair is it to judge God based on other people's evil destructive behavior. Free will, the hearts of men and the invisible evil presence around us continue to influence some very bad decision makings that can ultimately impact our perception of God in a negative way.

It takes much effort, dedication and a great deal of faith to be able to draw close to our maker. If anyone can attest to that, I surely can. In the early stages of my reformation I had a hard time with prayer. Not only did I not know how to properly pray but I also struggled with actually feeling the prayer itself. It took consistency and a lot of persistence in the beginning for me to feel the way I do today and that deep connection with God. More often than not I had to push through my feelings of doubt, shame and uncertainty in the beginning but God kept reassuring me with his support and acceptance throughout the process. When our Father sees perseverance and desperation with trying to stay connected with him, he will relentlessly try to keep that relationship going whether we realize it or not. We are his precious creation, like a father to a child, he wants us talking to him and for us to run to him for comfort.

Unfortunately, society seems to be quite wrapped up in satisfying their own comfort and convenience and will not take on complex dedications or such commitment to make that connection with Christ. When confronted with responsibility to pursue Him, some will often feel guilty about not knowing how to begin. It is human nature to try to avoid uncomfortable feelings which can critically delay the efforts to seek Him. I have even heard the excuse "I believe in all religions as long as it betters a person, therefore, there is not only one right religion". That's like saying, any kind of medication can cure diabetes, as long as it's for a good cause. Doesn't make sense, does it?

Just like the safety helmets we wear to safeguard our head from injury, insulated gloves to shield our hands from the cold, or boots we slip on to protect us from the murky rain and mud, we also need to protect our souls by emerging ourselves with the Holy Bible.

God has been more than generous with aspects to providing us with evidence of his divine authority, yet people still choose to turn away and reject his power. Such evidence has been provided by television shows, books or movies based on true stories, tributes and of course the bible, which is the greatest testimonial of all. Supernatural evidence has been and still is all around, however this is still not enough for our liking. Even in spite of a person being able to throw fire from their hand and levitate, it still wouldn't be enough to have a change of heart.

Most of us want to help our brothers and sisters out when the occasion arises, especially if it means saving others in the process. Its human nature to want to gossip and share exciting news and information with one another once its discovered. That is exactly what happened here, I couldn't wait to share the information and scream it to the world. Most importantly I want to warn other psychic mediums and make them aware of what happens when you play with the deceitful devil.

Utmost will be naive to the facts that I have presented in this book and some will even dismiss my encounters for a bad omen, but the truth of the matter is, judgement day comes for everyone. It's one thing to not believe if you haven't been exposed to the truth but when you have been shown evidence and still voluntarily make a decision not to believe, that is ten times worse than the one who never knew.

Unfortunately, such ignorance has existed with our previous and current generations, and will continue with our future generations. Humans have been blessed with the opportunity and the freedom to be able to make their own choices on a daily basis and everyday people are still choosing eternal death, not eternal life. Consciously they might not be aware of this until death and when judgement has finally come for them, but by that time, it might be too late. It doesn't necessarily mean that they are bad people, but the rule is same for all, one must believe and accept Jesus Christ as our savior in order to be able to enter into the kingdom of heaven and to attain eternal life.

There are a multitude of religions out there with many more to arise but none offers forgiveness and salvation with an everlasting life, only Jesus Christ does. No other Gods or deities offer such an up close and personal relationship like the one with the Father above. He makes himself available to us here on earth, right here, right now, any given moment with a click of a prayer. He is the most forgiving out of all prospers and always hopes to lead us home.

Other false and fake Gods, which don't even exist, demand bizarre rituals and materialistic offerings. The one true almighty God only requires our faithfulness and our steadfast love to be solely for him and no other before him. Not only do we learn to live righteously by doing this but we also get rewarded for our dedication, which is a forever life in a beautiful Kingdom called Heaven.

I have never been this happy and content with myself like I am now since my conversion. I wish that I had truly given God a chance earlier in my life but that time has come and gone. Why it took this long to finally answer his call is a combination of confusion, selfishness, doubt and lack of guidance. I am thankful that I am only in my forties and that hopefully I have a good amount of time left in my life to make up for the lost time with the Lord. I worry that I will be mocked and shunned upon with aspects to the contents of this book, but then I remember that this book wasn't my idea but God's and that if he bought me to it and through it, he will surely use it for his will. He will work his magic and land the book on the laps of people that need to read it the most.

ABOUT THE AUTHOR

Beatrix Szanto was born in Hungary, Budapest in 1976, and migrated to the United States in 1985. She resides with her beautiful children and husband in Hartford, Connecticut.

She enjoys horseback riding and spending time with her family and friends.

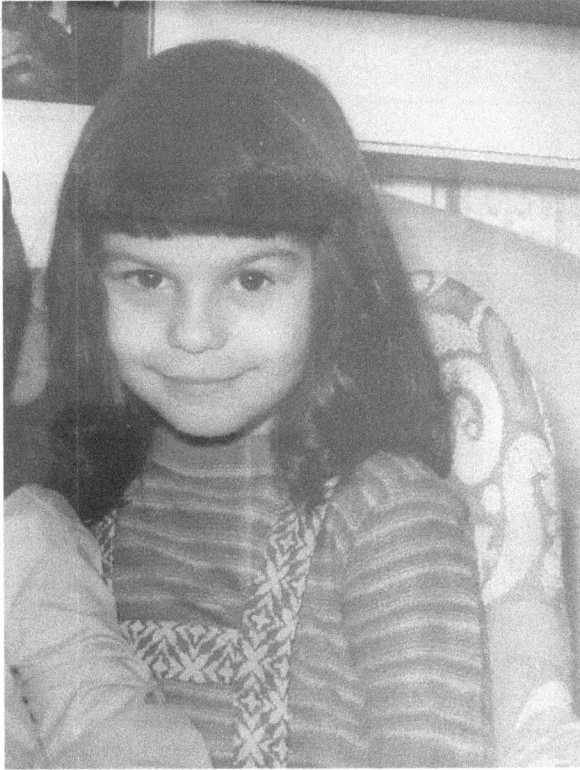

Picture of Beatrix Szanto at age 4 years in Budapest, Hungary.

Family photo.

www.ingramcontent.com/pod-product-compliance
Lightning Source LLC
Chambersburg PA
CBHW072040040426
42447CB00012BB/2946